Becoming a Disciple

Becoming a Disciple is translated from the French published by Éditions Olivétan as *Devenir Disciple.*

In the same collection of translations:

The Silence of God during the Passion

Praying the Psalms

Spiritual Maladies

The Tenderness of God

Repentance—Good News!

From Darkness to Light

Becoming a Disciple

Daniel Bourguet

Foreword by Bob Ekblad

Translated from the French

 CASCADE *Books* · Eugene, Oregon

BECOMING A DISCIPLE

Cascade Books
An Imprint of Wipf and Stock Publishers
199 W. 8th Ave., Suite 3
Eugene, OR 97401

www.wipfandstock.com

PAPERBACK ISBN: 978-1-4982-8167-6
HARDCOVER ISBN: 978-1-4982-8169-0
EBOOK ISBN: 978-1-4982-8168-3

Cataloguing-in-Publication data:

Names: Bourguet, Daniel.

Title: Becoming a disciple / Daniel Bourguet.

Description: Eugene, OR: Cascade Books, 2016.

Identifiers: ISBN 978-1-4982-8167-6 (paperback) | ISBN 978-1-4982-8169-0 (hardcover) | ISBN 978-1-4982-8168-3 (ebook)

Subjects: LSCH: Discipling (Christianity)—Biblical teaching | Spiritual formation | Christian life—Biblical teaching | Mystical union

Classification: BV4520 B68 2016 (PRINT) | BV4520 (EBOOK)

Manufactured in the U.S.A.   07/12/16

Contents

Translator's note

IN SOME INSTANCES THERE are idioms in French that are difficult to translate, but that has not generally been the case with this book. The author's original notes and references are all to French works or translations, and it has not always been possible to provide equivalent references in English. Further to the author's original notes some translator's notes have been added as footnotes, generally as glosses of the French, sometimes of a more explanatory nature; in every instance these notes have been checked with the author. Biblical passages are mostly the translator's version of the French, since at times the point would be lost if this were not so; the author chooses freely among French translations.

Foreword

THE PUBLICATION OF DANIEL Bourguet's books in English is a valuable contribution to the literature of contemplative theology and spirituality that will nourish and inspire the faith of all who read them. Daniel Bourguet, a French Protestant pastor and theologian of the Huguenot tradition, lives as a monk in the mountainous Cévennes region in the South of France. There at his hermitage near Saint-Jean-du-Gard, Daniel maintains a daily rhythm of prayer, worship, Scripture reading, theological reflection, and spiritual accompaniment. All of his books flow out of a life steeped in love of God, Scripture, and the seekers who come to him for spiritual support.

I first met Daniel Bourguet in 1988 when my wife, Gracie, and I moved from rural Central America to study theology at the Institut Protestant de Théologie (IPT), where he taught Old Testament. The IPT is the Église protestante unie de France's[1] denominational graduate school in Montpellier, France.

Prior to our move to France while ministering among impoverished farmers in Honduras in the 1980s, we had come across the writings of Swiss theologian Wilhelm Vischer and French theologian Daniel Lys by way of footnotes in Jacques Ellul's inspiring books. Vischer had written a three-volume work entitled *The Witness of the Old Testament to Christ*, of which only volume 1 is translated into English.[2]

1. Then the Église réformée de France.
2. Wilhelm Vischer, *The Witness of the Old Testament to Christ*, vol. 1, *The*

That book, along with a number of articles and Daniel Lys' brilliant *The Meaning of the Old Testament*,[3] exposed us to a community of Bible scholars who articulated a continuity between the Old and New Testaments that was highly relevant then and now. This connection would ultimately lead me to Bourguet.

We experienced firsthand how a literal reading of the Old Testament in isolation from the New Testament confession that Jesus is both Lord and Christ (Messiah) brings great confusion, division, and even destruction. In rural Honduras churches often distinguish themselves by selective observance of Old Testament laws and use certain Old Testament stories to inspire fear of God as punishing judge. In North America Christians were drawing from the Old Testament to justify the death penalty and US military intervention in Central America and beyond.

Wilhelm Vischer himself had been an active resister of Nazism from his Old Testament teaching post inside Germany. He resisted the misuse of Scripture to justify anti-Semitism, nationalism, and war, insisting on the importance of the Old Testament for Christian faith at a time when it was being dismissed. He was consequently one of the first professors of theology to be pressured to leave his post and eventually depart Nazi Germany before World War II, and served as Karl Barth's pastor in Basel after he too left Germany. After the war, the church in France, having been widely engaged in resistance to Nazism and deeply encouraged by Barth, invited Vischer to be the professor of Old Testament at the IPT in Montpellier.

Ellul, Vischer, Lys and other French theologians were offering deep biblical reflection that led us to look into theological study in France.[4] We wrote the IPT about their graduate program and

---

Pentateuch, trans. A. B. Crabtree (London: Lutterworth, 1949).

3. Daniel Lys, *The Meaning of the Old Testament* (Nashville: Abingdon, 1967).

4. We were able to study with pastor and New Testament professor Michel Bouttier, who was also trained by Vischer and published broadly, including a commentary on Ephesians and a number of collections of provocative articles. Elian Cuvillier followed Michel Bouttier and is currently Professor of New Testament at

discovered that Vischer had long since retired after training several generations of pastors. His protégée, Daniel Lys, had recently retired but was still available. In Lys' place was his doctoral student Daniel Bourguet, who also had been trained by Vischer. The IPT welcomed us with a generous scholarship and we were soon making plans to learn French and move to Montpellier.

We were eager for help to understand Scripture after being immersed in Bible studies with impoverished farmers in war-torn Honduras. Disillusioned with America after being engaged in resisting US policy in Central America, we felt drawn to reflect from a different context. We reasoned that studying in a Protestant seminary with a history of persecution in a majority Catholic context would prove valuable. We left Tierra Nueva in the hands of local Honduran leaders and moved to Montpellier two months early to study French and began classes in September 1988.

Daniel Bourguet taught us Hebrew and Old Testament in ways that made the language and text come alive. He invited students into his passion and curiosity as we pondered both familiar and difficult passages of Scripture. I remember continually being surprised at how seriously Daniel took every textual critical variant, even seemingly irrelevant ones. He masterfully invited and guided us to both scrutinize and contemplate each variant in its original language until we understood the angle from which ancient interpreters had viewed the text. Daniel modeled an honoring of distinct perspectives as we studied the history of interpretation of each passage. He sought to hold diverse perspectives together whenever possible, yet only embraced what the text actually permitted, exemplifying fine-tuned discernment that inspired us.

Daniel's thorough approach meant he would only take us through a chapter or two per semester. This meant we took entire courses on Genesis 1-2:4, on Abraham's call in Genesis 12:1-4, and on Jeremiah 31, Exodus 1-2, Psalms 1-2 and others. In each of his courses he

the IPT, writing many high quality books and articles.

included relevant rabbinic exegesis, New Testament use of the Old Testament, and the church fathers' interpretations. Daniel imparted his confidence that God speaks good news now as he accompanied us in our reading, making our hearts burn like those of the disciples on the road to Emmaus—and inspiring us to want to do this with others. In alignment with Vischer and Lys he demonstrated through detailed exegesis of Old Testament texts how God's most total revelation in Jesus both fulfills and explains these Scriptures, making them come alive through the Holy Spirit in our lives and diverse contexts.

While living in France every summer Gracie and I traveled from France to Honduras, spending several weeks sharing our learning with Tierra Nueva's Honduran leadership and leading Bible studies in rural villages before returning back for classes in the Fall. We had pursued studies in France with the vision of bringing the best scholarship to the service of the least in a deliberate effort to bridge the divide between the academy and the poor. Our experience of the rare blend of scholarship and pastoral sensitivity, which you will see for yourself in his books, contributed to us feeling called back to the church, into ordained ministry and back to the United States to teach and minister there. I benefited from his being my dissertation supervisor as I continued to integrate regular study into our ministry of accompanying immigrants and inmates as we launched Tierra Nueva in Washington State.

Daniel Bourguet's writings are like high-quality wine extracted from vineyards planted in challenged soil. Born in 1946 in Aumessas, a small village in the Cévennes region of France, Daniel Bourguet grew up in the heartland of Huguenot Protestantism, which issued from the Reformation in the sixteenth century. He pursued studies of theology at the IPT in Montpellier, including study in Germany, Switzerland and at the Ecole Biblique in Jerusalem. In lieu of military service, Daniel served as a teacher in Madagascar. He was ordained as a pastor in the Église réformée de France in 1972, serving parishes from 1973 to 1987. Daniel wrote his doctoral dissertation[5] while serving as

---

5. See Daniel Bourguet, *Des métaphores de Jérémie*, Paris : J. Gabalda, 1987.

a full-time parish pastor—a common practice in minority Protestant France, where teaching positions are scarce and pastors are in high demand. This practice often proves fruitful for ordinary Christians and theologians alike, deepening reflection and anchoring theologians in the church and world.

During our residential studies in Montpellier from 1988 to 1991, Gracie and I witnessed Daniel's interest in the early monastics and fathers of the Eastern church. In 1991 Daniel became prior of La Fraternité Spirituelle des Veilleurs (Spiritual Fraternity of the Watchpersons) and felt called to be a full-time monk, leaving the IPT in 1995 for a year in a Cistercian monastery in Lyon before moving to his current site in Les Cévennes in 1996.

Joy, simplicity, and mercy are the three pillars of Les Veilleurs, an association of laypeople and pastors founded by French Reformed pastor Wilfred Monod in 1923 (with a Francophone membership of four hundred in 2013). Members of this fellowship commit to pursuing daily rhythms of prayer and Scripture reading, including noontime recitation of the Beatitudes, Friday meditation on the cross, regular engagement with a faith community on Sundays, and spiritual retreats and reading that benefits from universal devotional and monastic practices. Les Veilleurs has served to nourish renewal in France and influenced the founding of communities such as Taizé. Under Daniel Bourguet's leadership Les Veilleurs thrived. As a member of Les Veilleurs I attended many of his annual retreats, witnessing and experiencing the vitality of this movement firsthand.

Daniel Bourguet's teaching and writing since his departure from his professorship at the IPT in 1995 have focused primarily on equipping ordinary Christians to grow spiritually through engaging in devotional practices such as prayer, Scripture reading and contemplation. Other works that will hopefully appear in English include reflections on asceticism, silence, daily prayer and the trinity. All but three of Daniel's twenty-five or so books are based on his spiritual retreats offered to pastors and retreatants with Les Veilleurs. He has offered retreats to

Roman Catholic, Orthodox, and Protestant communities throughout France and Francophone Europe and is widely read and appreciated as a theologian who bridges divergent worlds and nourishes faithful Christian practice in France. Daniel Bourguet made his first and only visit to the United States in 2005, offering a spiritual retreat in Washington State. He accompanied me to Honduras on that same trip just after Hurricane Katrina ravaged the country, teaching Tierra Nueva's leaders and accompanying me as I led Bible studies and ministered in rural communities.

Daniel left his role as prior in 2012 and now continues his daily offices, receives many seekers for personal retreats, and offers occasional retreats where he lives and writes. In alignment with the early monastic commitment to manual labor, Daniel weaves black and white wool tapestries of illustrations of Biblical stories done by pastor and painter Henri Lindegaard. Daniel's unique contribution includes his Trinitarian approach to biblical interpretation wherein he reads Scripture informed by the early church fathers, with special sensitivity to how texts bear witness directly but also indirectly to Jesus, the Father and the Holy Spirit.

Daniel Bourguet models an approach to Scripture and spirituality desperately needed in our times. He reads the Bible with great confidence in God's goodness, discovering through careful reading, prayer, and contemplation insights that feed faith and inspire practice. Daniel's deliberate reading in communion with the church fathers brings the wisdom of the ages to nourish the body of Christ today. His tender love for people who come to him for spiritual support, and the larger church and world inform every page of his writing, inspiring like practice. May you find in this book refreshment, strength, and inspiration for your journey as you are drawn into deeper encounters with God.

Bob Ekblad

Mount Vernon, WA
July 7, 2016

Preface

THIS BOOK REPRISES STUDIES given in the course of the year 2004 during a series of retreats of the Fraternité Spirituelle des Veilleurs, as well as other retreats, such as those at Crêt Bérard in Switzerland or Chimay in Belgium. In retreats, as with preaching, bibliographic references are left to one side; they might have had a place in marginal notes, but I have preferred to keep them to a minimum in order to stay close to the style of a retreat, as if the reader had also been invited to take part in a retreat through this book.

The people present at these retreats were believers, Christians, and the reader will see that my remarks assume this. Nothing has been changed here, so a reader who is not a believer will undoubtedly feel uncomfortable at times; for the host of questions that will arise for such a reader I ask pardon; however, to go on a retreat is to retire from the world for a time to be face to face with God, and the teaching at a retreat is a means to that encounter; for this, a person would have to be a believer. You need to know this before starting to read the book; I am speaking here as if at a retreat, to a reader who is a believer.

Finally, again as if on a retreat, I have kept the elements of an oral style. You are addressed here as a "reader friend," in the form of a dialogue, a dialogue that doesn't propose to be more than an overture to the most sublime of dialogues, that with God.

So there we are, my reader friend! May your dialogue with God find something here to nourish it.

— CHAPTER 1 —

Come, Follow Me

After John had been handed over, Jesus came to Galilee, preaching the gospel of God. He was saying, "The time is accomplished and the kingdom of God is at hand. Repent and believe the gospel."

As he was passing along the shore of the sea of Galilee, he saw Simon and Andrew, Simon's brother, who were casting their net into the sea, because they were fishermen. Jesus said to them, "Come and follow me, and I will make you fishers of men." And immediately, leaving their nets, they followed him.

When he had gone a little further, he saw James, the son of Zebedee, and John, his brother, who were also in a boat, repairing their nets. Immediately he called out to them; and, leaving their father Zebedee in the boat with the workers, they left and followed him. (Mark 1:14–20)

Preaching with no response

WHEN JESUS ARRIVED IN Galilee to begin preaching, according to Mark's Gospel he had not yet pronounced a single word. His ministry had begun on the banks of the Jordan, at the time of his baptism, but on that particular day he was entirely silent (1:1–11). Next, in the wilderness, where he was tempted for forty days by the devil, he, again, never said a thing (1:12–13). Curiously, Jesus' ministry begins with a deep silence, a silence so impressive indeed that a reader of the Gospel, intrigued by it, begins to thirst for what Christ will say; we are being prepared to receive the first words that will issue from his mouth with the highest degree of attention.

What then were these first words? It was preaching, and not just any preaching; "he preached the gospel of God," Mark tells us. Thus is Christ's first preaching designated! The content is presented as coming from God himself, and as being for its part a "gospel," which is to say, good news addressed to people. It is difficult to know what more could be done to indicate the importance of this preaching.

Each theme within what was preached can be made the subject of lengthy commentaries: the fullness of time, the closeness of the kingdom of God, repentance, faith in the gospel . . . . Each word is weighted with gold and would be the worthy subject of a retreat, but it is not on any of this that I wish to dwell, not at this moment.

We see, then, that Mark underlines the importance of Jesus' first preaching very carefully, but curiously, he forgets to tell us to whom it was addressed. Was it in a synagogue? In a public place? Beside the lake? On a mountain . . . ?

Mark also forgets to tell us how the preaching was received. No reaction on the part of the audience is told us! It's as if Jesus had preached in a wilderness! No one seems to have been touched, interested, or challenged! It looks as though the good news of God leaves the world indifferent! Is this not, in the end, how it is? Isn't this the sad truth, as John the Evangelist for his part notes—"He came to his own but his own received him not!" (John 1:11). How impoverished we are!

God searches for people

How true it is; no one is really interested in God! No one is truly preoccupied with God! No one truly seeks him! On the contrary, from the beginning of the world, God has unceasingly sought man—man, who is at the heart of his love. "Where are you?" God calls as he goes looking for Adam, as for a lost sheep (Gen 3:9). It's in just the same way that Jesus, after his first, unremarked preaching, goes in search of men and women, looking for each of his lost sheep. He sets off for the shore of the sea of Galilee and begins by calling two of them, then two others, and so on right down, doubtless, to you and me . . . .

There is a preliminary truth here we do well to recognize; it is not, in fact, we who seek God. If we have now become disciples, it is not the result of our own seeking, our own quest for God, but because of *his* initiative. It is he who has come to meet us, to call us. We are each of us lost sheep whom he is at pains to seek. He invites us to follow him. "You would not have sought me if I had not already found you," Christ said to Pascal; this is the truth for each of us.[1]

It is a little different in the other Gospels, but in Mark's it is clearly indicated that no disciple became such on their own initiative. The few individuals who proposed themselves did not in the end follow Christ; they all became discouraged, the best-known example being the rich young man of Mark 10:17–22. On the contrary, all those who truly followed Jesus were beneficiaries of his initiative.

Here, beside the lake, Jesus is come to seek the first four disciples. Later, the same happens with Levi; Levi does not initiate following Jesus; instead Jesus comes to his tax collecting booth to invite him to follow him (2:14). When it comes to Philip, the account of his calling, as told in John's Gospel, is still more suggestive: "Jesus found Phillip and said to him, 'Follow me!'" (1:43). The use of the verb "find" is very significant; it shows that Jesus had surely been searching for Philip. It is not that Philip found Jesus after searching for him . . . and it is just the same for each of us; whoever is a disciple must know that Jesus sought and found them, and that, through Jesus, it is God who seeks us and finds us.

---

1. Blaise Pascal (1623–62), prominent mathematician, thinker, spiritual author, well-known to French believers. (Trans.)

From darkness to light

Why these men, these four fishermen,[2] and not others? Were they particularly meritorious, worthy of being the object of Jesus' attention? The Gospel is silent on this point. Those who are called know very well at the bottom of their beings that they have no merit, that they have nothing to advance in the way of virtue, of personal dignity or aptitude, to be disciples.

In Luke's parallel account, Peter's reaction is still clearer on this: "Lord, depart from me, I am just a sinner" (5:8), he said as he threw himself down at Jesus' feet. By saying this, Peter indicates the gulf that separates him from Christ, the chasm, really, formed by sin. Depart from me, this chasm is impassable.

In his response, Jesus spans the impassable abyss with one sentence: "Fear not; henceforth you will be a fisher of men" (5:10).

When Peter opened his mouth to speak, it is not because Jesus had asked him anything but because, in the presence of the Lord, he felt his need. Jesus replies, but without the slightest curiosity as to the sin in question, without pressing for some confession, but with marvelous discretion: "Fear not!" Nothing can compromise my call. I know very well that you are a sinner, and that you are not worthy to be a disciple; but my word of love makes you worthy. It is not because of your merits but because of my grace that I am calling you.

In the Gospels, Jesus never inquires of those he is calling as disciples as to their past. He is not concerned about what their lives had been to that point. He asks no question. We go too far today when we seek to get new disciples to tell everything, even during the course of spiritual counselling. We often ask too many questions, and at times this borders on being indecent! There is nothing of this in the reserved attitude of Jesus. Not only Jesus, but the Gospels too, are extremely discreet about the disciples' pasts; it is enough just to

---

2. French has an interesting coincidence of words here. The word in the text for fisherman is *pêcheur*; the word for sinner is *pécheur*. (Trans.)

present their names: Andrew, Simon, James, John, Phillip, Levi . . . Just their names, which is to say, the deep mystery of their beings, their personhood before God. What good is there in speaking of the disciples' past when it is their future that matters?

Everything in our life truly begins with the encounter with Jesus. Whatever the darkness obscuring our past might be, his word causes light to rise upon us.

The word that gives birth to obedience

Where there is no description by Mark of the audience's reaction after Jesus' first occasion of preaching in Galilee, here by contrast, in the account of the first disciples' calling, their reaction is extraordinary: "Immediately they followed him."

Unlike Luke, Mark does not report any dialogue between Peter and Jesus. It is enough for him to report the common reaction of the fishermen, a reaction which comes into sharp focus: "Immediately they followed him."

What Jesus says is immediately put into effect. The men he has called obey without delay, without discussion, without hesitation, unquestioningly!

I must confess, reader friend, that for a long time I was very impressed by the reaction of these first four disciples, full of admiration for these men so exemplary in their obedience. They hear one word and ask for nothing, no sign, no miracle, no assurance, no guarantee! They hurry to obey! For a long time my interest was solely in them until I realized that I had my priorities wrong. What should attract our attention is not the disciples, but Jesus. What is so impressive and admirable is not them but him and him alone.

What follows in Mark's account, moreover, helps us reestablish this correct outlook. In the following verses the crowd is also full of admiration, very impressed, but by whom? By Jesus, not by the disciples!

The attention of the crowd is fixed on Jesus, not on the four Galileans behind him. The thing that strikes the crowd is not the obedience of the first disciples but the authority of Jesus, the power of his word: "They were amazed because he taught as one having authority" (1:27). "No one ever spoke like this man," as some of the officers attached to the rulers would later say (John 7:46). At no moment do the Gospels become excited about the disciples' obedience!

In reality, what is so admirable is not that the men should have left their boats, their work, their surroundings, their profession, and even that they should have "left all" as Peter would later say (Mark 10:28). What is so fine is the "authority" of Jesus, that is to say, the power of his word, which could snatch men away from their daily round, turn their lives upside down, and give them a new meaning. Nothing is said of the four Galileans' predisposition to obedience, of their aptitude for listening, the emotions they felt at Jesus' call. What is advanced is the authority, the power of Jesus' word. It was enough that he say, "come, follow me" and they came at once. What Jesus says is so strong that it is "immediately" put into effect. The important thing is not the obedience, but the word that gives birth to it.

Who then is this man to speak in this way with such authority? My attention, reader friend, has slowly moved away from the four obedient disciples towards the Master, whose word gives birth to obedience, firstly on the part of two unknown Galileans, then again on the part of two more, then again a little later, from unclean spirits in the Capernaum synagogue, to the great astonishment of the crowd: "What is this? What authority! He commands even the unclean spirits and they obey him!" (1:27)

The authority in fact of God's word

What then is this power in Christ, in his word? The remainder of the Gospel clarifies the issue little by little. We perceive as we go on in our reading that what happens with the first four disciples is the same as what happens to so many others, and even to the elements of creation: Jesus orders the sea to be still and it is, the wind to die down and it does (4:39); he even commands the demons to come out and they leave (1:25–27). He eventually orders a dead man to come forth from his tomb and the corpse emerges (John 11:38–44). Who then is he to speak with such authority?

Things work with Jesus exactly as for the one who, at the beginning of the world, said "let there be light," and light was. For his part, what the psalmist underlines with regard to God applies perfectly to Jesus: "He speaks and it is! He commands and it comes to pass!" (Ps 33:9). The power of Jesus' word is the same power as that of God. What is this? Jesus couldn't be God, could he? I believe this is the line of questioning Mark wishes to promote as we read his account, an account he refines to the maximum degree so as to confront us with the essential. "He said, 'Come, follow me,' and they immediately came and followed him!" Mark does not preach about the disciples but about Christ, to let us understand that he is God—his words produce the same effects as God's.

The miracle of obedience

In Luke's parallel account, Peter's calling is accompanied by a miraculous catch (5:1–11). Luke reports the miracle in a way that accords even greater authority and credit to Jesus as he invites followers. When Peter eventually follows him, this is because he has witnessed a catch that is out of the ordinary. In Mark's account it is quite different; Jesus still accomplishes a miracle, but the miracle in question is not the catch, but the obedience of Peter and Andrew, and then again that of James and John—as well as Levi's later . . . and then on to our day, in so many disciples. Each time someone becomes a disciple and follows Jesus, it is a miracle worked by Jesus, a miracle as great as the resurrection of someone from the dead. Moreover, this is just what Mark suggests in his account of Levi's calling. He "rose up" from his tax collectors desk (2:14), like Lazarus from his tomb. The verb "to rise up" used for Levi is the same verb used for the resurrection. Levi was therefore like a dead man until Jesus called him. The miracle is the effect of Jesus' word, which causes an entrance into life, true life, the life of God.

Reader friend, you who have become a disciple of Christ, you who march in his train, is not your obedience to the word of Christ, at the end of the day, a true miracle? We can take no glory from it when we obey! We should rather marvel to see how wonderfully the word of the Son of God has had its impact upon us, how it has brought us into life.

Vocation without discussion

In the accounts of vocation we find in the Old Testament, most of them contrast with the calling of the disciples on one very interesting point. There, those who were called by God dared to discuss things with him before they obeyed. In just this way, Moses asked a whole series of questions and expected answers from God, even though he stood before the miracle of the bush that burned without being consumed (Exod 3). He was called by God himself, and yet Moses dared to put forward objections! God had ordered him to remove his sandals and not to ask questions, but the lowly shepherd ventured to cross-examine the Lord of heaven and earth! His calling strongly resembles horse trading; the man engages in bargaining with God before obeying him! Jeremiah, for his part, also objected (1:6) and wanted signs before he would obey. When it comes to Jonah, he was happy just to run, without responding to God with so much as a word (1:3) before finally, after all his adventures, he too gave way. Ezekiel, although given an extraordinary heavenly vision, turned a deaf ear for a lengthy period before he too bowed to the authority of God . . . .

In the passage that concerns us, the disciples' obedience is immediate, which serves only to underline the great authority of Jesus' word; no bush burned beside the lake, nor did the heavens open to extraordinary visions! The disciples didn't dispute, ask any questions, or make so much as a single objection, though they would have had every right to do so; the unknown[3] standing before them had nothing to distinguish him from other men, only his word, in which there lay such power that every objection disappeared and every disobedience was excluded; they left everything and followed him!

Such is the power of Jesus' word, engendering obedience.

The power of love

What then is the nature of Christ's power? What lies behind the power of his word? There do indeed exist tyrannical powers, arbitrary powers, the power of evil, powers to charm . . . . It is enough to pronounce the name of Hitler to be aware of how the power of words can be malevolent, deadly to those who obey them. What is the nature of Christ's power? Mark says nothing, or rather he delays saying anything, and so brings us to an understanding with greater finesse. It is good to pause here a little on this aspect of his Gospel.

Before Jesus spoke a single word to the disciples, Mark tells us, he began by "looking" at them. The account is sufficiently bare that the mention of Jesus looking cannot escape our attention, still less when it is repeated: Jesus "sees" Simon and Andrew, then he speaks to them (v. 16). The same thing follows in that he "sees" James and John, and then he calls them (v. 19). Again, it is the same thing with Levi; Jesus "sees" him at his desk, and then calls him to follow him (2:14). Jesus' call seems to be inseparable from his having "looked." Is there any doubt

---

3. In all that follows, the author's attention is purposefully focused on the calling of the disciples solely as it appears in Mark, without reference to the other accounts. (Trans.)

that there is the same power in his look as in his word? Nevertheless, Mark reveals nothing further on this subject, simply because it touches on a certain modesty and this needs to be respected.

Mark waits until the tenth chapter of his Gospel to lift the veil a little. He does this on the occasion of an event that has all the hallmarks of someone being called, except that this is a failed vocation! The passage in question tells of the encounter between Jesus and the rich young man. When Jesus found himself in this man's presence and invited him to follow him and become his disciple, Mark tells us that Jesus began by looking at him intently. The look and the call are again closely connected. It is then that Mark interposes between the mention of the look and the call a simple verb, without any commentary, as discreetly as possible: "having observed him intently, he loved him and said to him, 'Follow me'" (10:21).

This is the strength behind Christ's look—*love*. Mark says nothing more!

To draw the reader's attention a little more to the love of Christ, Mark's sole recourse was to alter the verb used to designate how Jesus looked. On this occasion he does not use the simple verb "see" he had used with the first disciples but another one, more precise and stronger; this can be translated as "look inside" or "observe fixedly and deeply" (*emblepein*). Christ's look of love is so intense, so penetrating that it gets right to the core of the soul without being in the least prying or indiscreet; it is purely a look of love.

It is, it seems to me, in contemplating an icon of Christ that we can best perceive, with no need of any commentary, the inexpressible power of the Lord's look.[4]

Love; this then is the strength of how Christ looks at us, and it is also the power behind his word; a power that it is impossible to measure, it goes so far beyond anything we can say. The miracle of his word, the miracle of our obedience, is the miracle of his love for us. His love is such, indeed, that it doesn't seem possible for us to disobey him.

---

4. Some icons seem to look deep inside you. (Trans.)

Beside the sea of Galilee, the disciples perceived in Jesus' eyes and in his word such a power of love that it brought them to a state of silence, and they then obeyed. When love is so great, it does reduce us to silence. There is nothing to say. Leaving everything, the disciples followed Jesus . . . .

When the rich young man decided to disobey, it was because the door to his heart was locked tight by the love of money; he was still attached to the money. Obeying Christ means not resisting; it means opening the door to his love, allowing his love to conquer our heart.

All this can be of great utility to us. When we feel demands being made on us, how can we know if this comes from God? We will know with certainty when we can say with the Emmaus road disciples, "Did not our hearts burn while he spoke to us?" (Luke 24:32). At God's calling, the heart burns without being consumed, as the bush burnt before Moses! Even if our sick heart burns only feebly, this burning is different from a thousand others. When love begins to inflame our hearts, there are no questions to ask of Christ, no objections to offer, no remarks to be made, since they all disappear in that fire, not the fire of our love for Christ, but the fire of his love for us. This is the true fire which sets a life ablaze.

One greater than a prophet is here

Before speaking to the disciples, Jesus does not even go to the bother of introducing himself! It is amazing! He is completely unknown to them; no detail in the Gospel suggests that these four fishermen had heard any rumor of Jesus' opening preaching. On the day of his baptism, on the banks of the Jordan as Mark presents it, there were none but Judeans with John (Mark 1:5);[5] not one Galilean had accompanied

5. That is, John the Baptist. While this does not take account of John's Gospel (1:37–42), this, again, is because the author is focusing on Mark's evident intent. (Trans.)

Jesus, and neither had any Galilean anything to do with what ensued in the wilderness during the days of Jesus temptation.

Although, for Mark, he was altogether unknown to the four fishermen, Jesus says nothing about himself, puts forward nothing that would accredit him as a messenger of God. The prophets, before him, had spattered their discourses with characteristic formulae that would signal them in this way: "Thus says the Lord," "the oracle of the Lord," "the word of the Lord came to me, saying . . . ." There is nothing of this from Jesus! At no point in the Gospel does Jesus employ such phrases. He had no need for any authentication of his word because the power behind it is enough. In truth there is more to him than a prophet; he is the very Word of God, the Word made flesh; he is God. He speaks and it comes to pass. What need is there for signs, proofs, attestations, justifications, miracles? Surely his unfathomable love suffices?

The word of Christ is not a word that requires extraordinary lives to find a home, but a word that transforms ordinary lives and leads them into the extraordinary. It is not a word that is received by saints, but a word that lights a fire of God's love; not a word that manipulates and estranges, but a word that fashions lives so that they become what they are called to be, those of new creatures. It is not a word that can be measured by human standards, but one that conforms to God's.

Astonishing disobedience

I mentioned earlier how in my younger days I marveled at the obedience of the disciples, wondering how it could be that these men were so obedient. My question today is quite different: how can it be that there are those who do not obey? What is extraordinary is not obedience to the Son of God, but that we should disobey him.

Lord Jesus Christ, Son of God, the heavens and earth prostrate themselves before you. The sun and the stars obey your commands; the wind and the sea cannot resist your word; the beasts of the field and the birds in the air are submitted to your will; even unclean spirits bow at your word and a legion of demons are no obstacle to your instructions. But we, Lord, in our straying, we dare to disobey you! Who are we to dare behave in this way towards you? What pretension, what pride, could so perturb our spirit and make us this insensible?

My child, Christ responds to us, you are alone in what I have given you as opposed to every other visible creature. The sun and the moon have no ability to disobey me, no more than do the wind and the sea. You, however, can, since it is to you that I gave liberty; loving you means to love you by giving you freedom to obey me or disobey me! Your greatness is the greatness of your liberty, and the greatness of my love for you. By loving you, I run the risk of your disobedience, so that your obedience might be the free response of your love. No obedience could be greater in my eyes than yours, because yours is the expression of your freedom, of your free love.

"Come, follow me," says Jesus with all the strength of his love. Four Galilean fishermen, in complete liberty, leave their boats and follow him . . . . What a wonder! What a miracle of a love that attracts so powerfully!

A word and a project

To the call Jesus addressed to the disciples, Jesus adds a project: "I will make you fishers of men." At first sight we might think that it was this project that attracted the disciples, as rabbits are attracted to carrot! But that is quite wrong! The new profession Jesus was proposing was not a dream job including either a castle in Spain or a beachfront villa in Florida! It has no place in any chamber of commerce list of careers! "A fisher of men" conforms to no known job description! Not even a fisher of fishes could imagine what it might mean! Not in Galilee, nor any other sea in the world, were there fishers of men. And a search through the Old Testament throws up nothing comparable.[6]

When the disciples obey, it is not because they covet the task Jesus was proposing, nor because they were curious to discover this strange work, but because it was *Jesus* who proposed it; therefore it would all unfold as they followed, together with him.

The important thing about this project is that it was Jesus' idea, not the disciples'. We do not become disciples to realize our own projects, however beautiful they might be. Neither do we join the church in order to fulfill our own dreams. What a sadness to hear a young candidate for some ministry being asked, "What are your plans?" Happy is that one who knows to reply: "I have none, but Christ has one for me and that is what I seek to respond to, to the best of my ability and in the power of the Spirit!"

There is no need for a personal plan to set about following Christ; the issue is entering into *God's* plan. Any other plan can actually eclipse God's, hide it, and feed off it parasitically.

Frozen lives set in motion

The first effect of Christ's calling is that it sets the men in motion; the disciples follow him. Jesus' word is powerful enough to cause men to "get out of the boat"; they leave and follow Christ. The change brought about by Christ's word is purposeful; the disciples follow someone who is going somewhere definite. From the outset of Mark's Gospel, Jesus is always moving, going forward. He leaves Galilee for the Jordan; the moment he is baptized he comes up out of the water and goes into the wilderness; he re-emerges after forty days and returns to Galilee. At the lake he goes along the shore from boat to boat, and then pursues a route towards Capernaum and then other villages . . . . The one who

---

6. A theme that approaches this appears in Jer 16:16, but in another context in which the image is one relating to a plague, a calamity.

calls does not even have a place to lay his head; he is unceasingly in motion. The disciples, by following him, enter this constant movement. To be a disciple is to enter into Christ's movement, into his onward momentum, which from all time and for all time is a surging force of love. To be a disciple is to enter into Christ's onward surge of love.

To underline how the disciples are set in motion, Mark takes pains to describe them in a striking pose of immobility at the moment Jesus calls them. James and John are to be found in their boat repairing nets, an activity requiring stillness and concentration. When it comes to Peter and Andrew, they have the appearance of being a little more active as they throw their net into the sea. In fact though, this is really not so. To indicate that their act is one of great lassitude, Mark allows himself to commit an error in his Greek. "To throw a net" in Greek is a verb of movement which normally needs to be followed by a particle with an accusative to show that it is indeed a movement. Here, curiously, Mark has the verb for "throw" followed by a particle with a dative (*en tē thalassē*—in the sea), to show clearly that the action, contrary to appearances, is without movement, a single, paused image. This act of the two fishermen is as still as their lives; still as a life with no tomorrow, in which each day resembles the next. Mark harries the grammar into stating the unspoken fact of a life frozen in time.

Before Jesus calls the disciples, their lives, then, are fixed, always the same, with no tomorrow. With Jesus' call everything becomes movement, activated by the same movement in the life of Christ.

When Matthew comes to write his account of the calling of the first disciples, he does not presume to reproduce the "grammatical fault" of Mark; he corrects, using irreproachable Greek: "they were throwing a net into the sea" (*eis tēn thalassan*, Matt 4:18). Did Mark commit a basic grammatical fault? No, indeed. Mark had simply understood and wished to give expression to the energy of Christ, the movement into which he draws us; this is so extraordinary that to convey it he needed to somewhat bend the rules of the language.

The view from behind _____

If the Lord invites us to enter his momentum, his movement, where is he taking us? What is the goal to which he is leading us? Just to be in motion is not in itself a goal!

Before responding to this, I believe we should first take some time to meditate the fact of falling in behind Christ, following someone who is himself pressing forward. To follow someone like this means, essentially, seeing him from behind. We might for a time burn with the thought of a face-to-face encounter with Christ, and in the case of such an encounter any idea of movement would be irrelevant. But encounter like this may belong to the future when there is no longer a question of going forward, of following; however, at this point the issue is different, so we do not yet see his face, but see him only from behind. There was the occasion when Moses asked to see God face to face, and his request was refused! As an alternative, he was privileged to have God simply pass in front of him, to see him, even though it was only his back (Exod 33:23)! To participate in God's movement means observing him from behind. Who could see him face to face and remain alive, withstanding the intensity of his gaze? It is the same with Christ because he is God! We must begin by marching in his train, seeing him only from the back . . . . The face-to-face encounter is not yet for today![7]

We must however take up our question: Where is he going? What is the goal? The opening of Mark's Gospel (vv. 1–11) gives a wonderful reply to the question in the form of a superb paradox.

Towards the Father . . . _____

The baptism of Jesus indicates perfectly towards whom it is that Christ is directed, without it needing to be made explicit. In silence, Jesus

---

7. 1 Cor 13:12—"but *then* face to face." (Trans.)

comes up out of the water; it is then that the Spirit descends towards him. The Son and the Spirit move towards their mutual encounter in a profound silence. At this moment, the voice of the Father sounds down from heaven to meet the Son as he comes out of the water. The Son moves to meet the Father in the passion born of his desire for the Father's love. The Spirit descends, like the voice of the Father, towards the Son. It is all a movement of love among the Persons of the Trinity.

The Son, indwelt by this passion, is therefore simply leading us too into the same thing, towards the Father, towards the Holy Spirit. What a wonder! "Come, follow me," says Jesus simply. His words have the intensity of the infinite power of trinitarian love; the movement he draws us into is imbued with the ineffable grace of infinite love, the eternal dance of the Father, the Son, and the Holy Spirit. Contrasting with this grace, a fault in the Greek highlights the immobility of our lives, but then, how we are overturned by the sudden entrance of the word of God, drawing us into his activity!

"I am the way . . . ; no one comes to the Father but by me," says Jesus, using a turn of phrase that emphasizes movement (John 14:6). The Father is the goal of our onward march as we follow Christ, on the way that is Christ.

I think we need to consider an enormous objection, made very frequently these days, about these words, that Jesus should describe himself as *the* way, the only way! This phrase is objected to when it is misunderstood; considered as contentious when it is thought that there are roads other than Christianity that lead to God. This is a real objection; inter-faith dialogue makes modern people aware of a diversity of spiritual ways. This word of Jesus, however, says something else, going much further. Jesus does not say that he leads to God, but to "the *Father.*" This is not a man who leads us to God, but God the Son leading to God the Father. Jesus is not some master of thought, not the founder of a religion that leads us to God, but God leading us to God, the Son conducting us to the Father, into the heart of the Trinity. In this sense, in the very heart of the Trinity, Jesus is indeed the only one who can say, "No one comes to the Father but by me!" If we overlook the profound trinitarian nature of John's Gospel, this saying of Jesus is indeed contentious; it even seems incomprehensible and unacceptable; when we bear in mind this trinitarian aspect, contention is put away.

. . . and towards other people

We now turn back to the Gospel of Mark, which, alongside the account of the baptism, which opens onto the mystery of the Trinity, invites us to look at another direction in which Christ moves; this direction also needs to be considered if we are to understand the goal towards which the disciple is led as he walks in Jesus' footsteps.

When Christ came from Galilee to Jordan, it was another form of following in the ways prepared for him, just as John the Baptist had demanded in his preaching: "Prepare the way of the LORD!" (1:2). Each person is invited to prepare a way for the Lord, since the Lord comes to meet each one; it was to encounter the people that Jesus left Galilee. The meaning, the goal of his ministry is just that; throughout his life, and certainly beside the lake, Jesus went out in front of his people; then he called them to follow him, and become "fishers of men," which surely is to set people in motion towards those who are to be caught. Whoever follows Christ follows him in the passion, which leads him towards others.

The paradox lies here in Christ's twin objective, others and the Father. It is not our place to choose, but just to follow Christ in his pursuit of the two goals; they are inseparable.

That said, it is only as we make our way towards the Father that we can truly encounter others. You will know, reader friend, how we can suffer as we see our involvements with others so superficial, so often resulting in misunderstandings, or just plain incomprehension. I believe this stems from the fact that we do not pray enough before meeting others; it is God who gives human relations their depth and truth, so it is indeed the case that, the closer we draw to God, the nearer we can draw to others. We are mistaken in wishing to encounter others if we don't do so through God; we go no further than the surface of things, without there being a true meeting. Also, however, it would be wrong to pass over meeting others and just seek encounter with God.

Only in Christ is it possible to live out this paradox; it is he who leads us into the depths of God's heart since he is God, but it is also he who leads us into the depths of the human heart since he is the true man, moving in a passion of love which pulls everything together.

"Come, follow me," says the Son, the Son of God and Son of Man . . . . They left their boats and followed him . . . .

To follow and to follow

The verb "follow" is fundamental to an understanding of a disciple's calling, for every disciple. To be a disciple surely means to follow Jesus. The verb is frequently employed in the Gospels, almost the same number of times in each; twenty-five in Matthew, nineteen in Mark, seventeen in Luke, and eighteen in John, if I am not mistaken.

As we read the Gospels, we note that there are many ways to follow Jesus, but two main ones: the way the disciples followed and the way the crowd followed (Matt 4:25; 8:1, etc.).

The crowd followed Jesus on their own initiative, out of curiosity, out of interest, or for other reasons, but always for a short time only; tomorrow was not in the picture. By contrast, no disciple followed Jesus on his own initiative. It was Jesus who called, and it was his initiative. The only reason to follow him has to do with the call, and when this is the case, there is nothing solely of the moment about it.

It may be that a disciple begins to follow only "from afar," as was the case with Peter, for example (Mark 14:54). The continuation of this account shows that this leads, sooner or later, to denial. The disciple may, then, prove as unfaithful as the crowd, but, if there is still hope that he may follow once again, it is thanks to the faithfulness of Christ in renewing his call as he did with Peter (John 21:19, 22). The freedom of the disciple may lead to denial, but the faithfulness of Christ is such that he continues to seek his faltering follower. Each renewed appeal contains pardon for the past failings, and reopens the way. The spirit of love in Christ tugs at each disciple, including the one who has reneged. "Do you love me?" says Christ to Peter after his denial (John 21:15–19). To the disciple, who responds positively, Christ repeats what he had said that first day, "Follow me," reigniting the fire of renewed passion. The disciple's faithfulness depends on the faithfulness of Christ.

I will make you _____

The force behind Jesus' word, his power, needs to be considered from another angle, which we will do well to examine.

"I will make you to be . . . ." In this expression, Jesus uses the word "make." He announces that he will work on his disciples to the point that he makes them something they are not yet. If the disciples become fishers of men, it will be because of Jesus' intervention and action upon them.

In biblical Greek the word "make" is very strong. It is a verb that includes the idea of creation, as appears very clearly in the first verse of Genesis: "In the beginning, God created the heavens and the earth," says the Hebrew text. In the Greek translation the verse becomes: "In the beginning God made the heavens and the earth." The Greek is not in any way softening the Hebrew, because the Greek for "make" includes the sense of "create."

It is with the intensity of this verb "make" that we are to understand Jesus statement, "I will make you . . . ." The power set in motion by Christ is a creative power. Jesus will make his disciples into new creatures. The one by whom all things in heaven and earth were created, will now exercise his creative power on his disciples.

Nonetheless, these new creatures, the work of the Son of God, do not come into existence out of nothing, but from the starting point of their old being. The whole theme of the old man and the new man is apparent here, and Mark brings this to the fore with two expressions he places side by side. Firstly, "they were fishermen," which is to say they were fishers of fish (v. 16); this is what the four Galileans were in the reality of their old being. They will "become fishers of men" (v. 17); this is what the four Galileans will be in so far as the new man is concerned, as a result of the creative intervention of Christ.

Christ's intervening role here is very evident in the movement from the verb "be" to the verb "become." What the disciples were, and had been unchangingly from generation to generation of fishermen, is now going to pass into another reality, which could only proceed from Christ, since without him it does not even exist; "fishers of men" is an unknown notion, having no meaning apart from Christ. It is only with Jesus as intermediary that one could become a fisher of men.

This "becoming" a disciple is a setting in motion, not on this occasion in terms of kilometers, at a geographical level, but an internal movement of the being, at the level of root identity.[8] To follow Christ means entering into a particular movement, a movement that is his, as we have said. This is specified here; this setting into motion is interior, in the depths of one's being. This is possible not through our own doing, but through that of Christ. In following Christ, we entrust ourselves to him, that he work in us with his creative power, that from an old creature[9] he make a new creature.

---

8. The French says "at the level of existence." (Trans.)

9. Some English translations of 2 Cor 5:17 speak of a new "creation"; "creature" preserves the French. (Trans.)

Becoming what he is _____

What is this new being, this new creature, that comes into existence through the creative word of Christ? As I have already said, when it comes to fishers of men, there were none; or, more exactly, there was one, just one who could serve as a model. He is not, in the end, far to seek because he is right there at work beside the sea of Galilee. Moreover, right before our eyes he is there to fish for four men! That is the miraculous catch; Jesus has trapped in his net his first four disciples. The fisher of men, the unique and true fisher of men—he is it!

What is it that the disciples are going to "become"? Fishers of men; that is to say, what Jesus already is. The disciples are going to become what Jesus is! This is fabulous. They are not going to become Jesus, which would be an alienation of being; they remain Peter, Andrew, James, John, with their own deep inalienable identity, but they will participate in the very ministry of the Son of God, in his being, and thus become what he is.

To participate in the being or nature of Christ is no small thing! It means participation in his divine/human existence. It means becoming what he is in the quality of being he shares with the Father and the Holy Spirit. He alone, Jesus, can "make" this happen in our lives. It is the most extraordinary miracle, but it is not realized in an instant right there beside the lake. It is altogether a "becoming" that starts there, a profound process that begins and stretches across the years of Jesus' ministry and still further. One does not become a disciple in an instant but over the course of time, through the course of a life, following Christ step by step. It is not our own work but that of Christ the creator, a wonderful adventure.

To participate in the being of Christ is to participate in the very being of God, the trinitarian God! To affirm this is to affirm something infinitely beyond ourselves! Nevertheless, the Bible does here authorize and permit us to advance a little further into this mystery, so that we can see a little more clearly.

The being of God

The verb "to be" for people, as for all other creatures, is a verb of state, a static verb. In God's case, and for him alone, it is a verb of movement. "To be," a verb of movement? This certainly goes beyond our normal linguistic categories, but that should not deter us.

The proper name of God, the "tetragram" as the Hebrew word is termed, composed as it is of four letters (YHWH), the name received by Moses before the burning bush, the unpronounceable name since too holy for impure lips, this name is formed from the ancient Hebrew verb for "to be," *hwh*. When God responds to Moses, "I am who I am" (Exod 3:14), he is not really giving his name, but rather indicating that indeed "to be, being" is the core of his name, his deep identity. From this comes, as a confession of faith, "he is"—YHWH.

The verbal form that makes up the tetragram, curiously for us, is not a form of the verb that is "perfective," but instead is "imperfective" (these are two temporal conjugations in Hebrew). The concretizing spirit of Greek philosophy would never have accepted such a way of speaking of God, but the Hebrew affirms that God belongs to the sphere of the unfinished, the sphere of the becoming, the never-ceasing-to-become, to the eternal, interior movement that belongs to his very person. The being of God is infinite movement. In him, the verb "to be" is truly a verb of movement. To become a participant in his being is to enter into this movement.

He was, he is, and he is to come

In biblical Greek, the tetragram was never properly translated, and in truth it could not be. This proper name of God is entirely absent from the New Testament, neither transcribed because not to be pronounced, nor translated, since the Greek verb for "to be" is insufficient, too static, inadequate, incapable of signifying the idea of movement. What was to be done? How was the proper name of God to be justly conveyed in the Greek of the New Testament?

The greater part of the New Testament authors were happy to follow the Septuagint of the Old Testament, as was the current usage of the period in Judaism, replacing the name with the title "Lord."

The Evangelist John, nevertheless, breaks the mold and in a truly inspired way. In fact, he ventured an original "translation," composed not of one word, but of three, since one alone would not do. Three words, three verbal forms, that together manage to convey as well as is possible the Hebrew name for God: "Who is, who was, and who is to come" (Rev 1:4). John, then, deployed the verb "to be" in the present and the past, but then adding to it, not the future form, but the verb "to come," to give the idea of motion, which is incompatible with the Greek verb for "to be." It is very fine in John and truly inspired to designate God in this way, naming him, yet still without stating the name, so as to respect the prohibition on pronouncing it!

"Who is, who was, and who is to come"; this is the name John reserves for God (Rev 4:8); for the Father, yes (1:4), but also for the Son (1:8), underlining that Christ is just as much God as is his Father.

The prologue to John

In a very wonderful way, John constructs the prologue to his Gospel around these three verbal forms, each of which he applies to Christ, thereby emphasizing his divinity at the same time as he sets forth the incarnation (v. 14). Thus, Christ is "the Word who *was* at the beginning" (v. 1); he is also the light who *comes* (v. 9), and the only Son who *is* in the bosom of the Father (v. 18). We therefore find, strategically placed at the two extremes and at the center of the prologue, the three expressions that together form the name of God. John wonderfully honors his Master's divinity.

John, indeed, goes just about as far as is possible with the Greek language, forcing it to say something that is beyond words, indicating that the being of Christ is a being in movement. In Greek, the verb "to be," in so far as it is a verb of state, cannot be followed by a particle with the accusative, since this is a property of verbs of movement.[10] Here, at the start of the prologue, John does not say that the Word "was near to God" with a dative[11] (*pros tō theō*), but that it was "near to God" with an accusative (*pros ton theon*). This subtlety, which is untranslatable for us, is a misuse of Greek, in that it makes of the verb "to be" a verb of movement; we might render it as "in the beginning the Word was in motion[12] towards God," which is to say that from the beginning, for all time, the Son was in this motion towards the Father.

In the same way, at the end of the prologue, John does not say that the Son is "*on* the bosom of the Father" in the same way that he says it elsewhere of the well-beloved disciple, who was "on the bosom of Christ" (13:23), using the dative, *en tō kolpō*; instead he is "*onto*" the bosom of the Father, with the accusative, *eis ton kolpon*, which again misuses the Greek, making the verb "to be" a verb of movement! The Son is on the bosom of the Father in such a way that he is both in movement towards the Father and on the bosom of the Father, a motionless motion, in the movement of eternal love. The very being of Christ, in that he is God, is a movement of infinite love.

---

10. E.g., *I go to the bank. To* here is the particle and in Greek the ending of the noun for *bank* would change (inflect) to show movement towards it, a meaning conveyed in English by the particle. (Trans.)

11. In highly inflected languages like Latin, Greek, and Russian, the dative noun ending indicates an indirect object, and does not suggest motion towards. (Trans.)

12. Here it is the French that defies translation. The word is *élan* and it conveys a complex of ideas with no English equivalent. (Trans.)

The disciple becomes a son _____

By making us become what he is, Christ causes us to participate in the eternal dance of love that is God's alone. Christ causes us to participate in the very being of God; he causes us to become "participants in the divine nature," as Peter puts it (2 Pet 1:4). This is what a disciple is, someone whom Christ has given to partake of God's very being and of his eternal grace of love . . . . What a wonder! He alone, assuredly can "make" such a thing be.

"Come, follow me," Jesus says, drawing his own after him on paths thitherto inaccessible to man, paths on which we become, by his grace, new creatures.

What we are discovering here with regard to our fishermen called to become fishers of men can be applied to the calling of every disciple, even though not all disciples are called to be fishers of men. There are a diversity of callings in the bosom of the church. Some are called to be pastors, others to become teachers, deacons, chaplains, hospital visitors, Sunday school officers, or something else again . . . each Christian, each disciple, is called to a particular service, but each time the deep, spiritual reality is the same; each disciple is called by the effective grace of Christ to become what he, Christ, is. Christ, truly, is all at once pastor, teacher, deacon, chaplain, hospital visitor, Sunday school officer . . . . From this it follows that each Christian is called to follow Christ in order to be turned into a participant in his being, to become what he is, by one means or another. The diversity of callings serves only to display the riches of the unique being of Christ. Each Christian in his calling lives out a facet of Christ's ministry.

In this diversity, a common reality is shared between all, that is, each Christian becomes a son or daughter, a child of God. What we all become is what he is, he, the Son of God. He is the only Son of God, and he does not become this, because he has been such from all eternity, in his very being. We, by contrast, we become by adoption, by grace, what he is by nature. We become this by sharing in his sonship, by participating in his being.

This difference between him and us appears clearly in various Gospel turns of phrase to which we do well to pay careful attention. On one hand, at the baptism, the Father says to Christ, "You are my Son" (Mark 1:11), which sets forth the essence of Christ, his filial essence. On the other hand, in Revelation, God says of the Christian, "He will be a son to me" (21:7), a formula of adoption, which points to what is to come; it is no longer *uios mou* which is reserved for Christ, but *uios moi*, with a dative that conveys the Hebrew equivalent of the verb "to become." Without us, Christ is always the Son; but without him, we can never become sons, since it is through him that it is possible, through him, the one who makes us participants in his being.

It is this reality of our being on the way to becoming that causes the apostle to rejoice; "My beloved, we are right now children of God, but what we shall be has not yet been made manifest. We know that when he appears, we shall be like him because we shall see him as he is" (1 John 3:2).

Continuity and rupture

"They were fishermen," and they will "become fishers of men." In this double formula of the Gospel account both continuity and change appear very clearly, and this also is part of the life of the disciple.

"They were fishers" and will stay "fishers"; this is continuity; but from fishers of "fish" they are to become fishers of "men," and this is the change. In each call, and in the life of each disciple, this twin reality is present. There is always a certain continuity in the existence of the disciple, in their particular abilities, but these are to be put to use in a different setting. Someone who is a musician, for example, will still be one, but their art will blossom in another way, in another reality of life, and for the good of the kingdom.

The change that alters the life of the disciple consists of abrupt change, rupture. We see it here, that to become fishers of men, the disciples no longer had need of their boat or nets, not even of Zebedee, their father, who as the professional fisherman was the one who had taught the boys their trade. Zebedee stayed in the boat with the workers and the nets because he remained a fisherman, while James and John left everything to become fishers of men. The break, the rupture with Zebedee is at a professional level rather than of family ties.

Why these ruptures? Because the disciples' new work makes it necessary. The disciples now need a different type of boat, a net of another kind, and a different master. The church fathers were bold, but, as I think, felicitously so in the way they develop this theme.

The boat and the net . . .

The new boat for the activity of fishing for men would be understood by the fathers as the church, and so it is. Church is not to be understood here in confessional terms, but the one universal church, which includes and goes beyond the institutional churches. It is into this universal church that those people snatched from the sea are brought; the sea, the place of death in biblical thought.

When it comes to the net used to fish, this is nothing other than the means Jesus used to catch those first four disciples; that is, his word. The men were drawn to Jesus by his word; he is a fisher of men by means of his word. Once again, we find here the idea of the power of the word; the word of Christ is powerful enough to snatch these four men away from the sea and their livelihoods.

The net to be used by the disciples is not their own word, but that of Christ working through them. The word of a disciple will never be able, on its own, to catch so much as a single soul. If it should be that a disciple's speech is strong enough to succeed, it's because we are talking about the word of Christ. The efficacy of human speech has to do with the fact that God inserts his own word into it. There is nothing automatic about this; the word of a disciple does not automatically contain in itself the word of God, but God in his grace, when and how he wishes, can give the disciple's word the power of his word. This miracle operates through the Holy Spirit.

The disciple has no other net than the word. There is something of a tendency these days to multiply contrivances intended to make Christian preaching attractive, forceful, and effective. There may be certain techniques, pedagogical strategies to be used alongside the word, and this is not so bad on condition that we do not forget that the word alone is the net that enables men to be caught.

. . . and the father

The boat, the net . . . but what of Zebedee? Who henceforth was to replace him, to be a trainer to the disciples in their new work of catching men? Who was to be their "father" in the professional sense? Jesus, of course. He alone could be a "father" to the disciples, to teach them the activity to which they were called. One Gospel passage causes the role attributed to Christ as "father" vis-à-vis the disciples to stand out very clearly.

After the resurrection, John's Gospel shows us the disciples in a boat on the sea of Galilee. They had gone back to their old trade, no doubt because bewildered by the death of their Master. The boat, the nets . . . everything was there, except Zebedee! They no longer had a father! Then we see how disastrous the fishing was; they were returning to shore empty handed. Next, though, an unknown figure appears on the shore and gives them an instruction that will prove excellent, showing that the unknown is one of them, a true professional when it came to fishing. "Throw the net to the starboard side of the boat," he told them (21:6), and there was a miraculous catch! Before he gave the order to the disciples, the unknown addressed them as "my children" (21:5). The father therefore is . . . Jesus!

Let's go back, though, to the account of the calling, when the disciples leave their boat, their net, and their father, Zebedee. Nothing of the nature of a rupture is actually demanded in the account by Jesus, but separation can be seen as the logical outcome of the call. The ruptures were implicitly contained within the call, and Jesus had no need to speak of them. It is not until later that Peter would affirm that he, when everything was taken into account, had left *everything* to follow Jesus (Mark 10:28).

Sometimes it can be preached that renouncement, separations, deprivations are an end in themselves, but this is a mistaken understanding. All of these take place in a disciple's life, but as logical, unavoidable consequences, implicitly, tacitly contained within the call.

To leave or to quit?

The Greek verb used at the moment the disciples respond to Jesus' call is very clear and it means "leave" and not "quit." Nowhere in the dictionaries is the sense of "quit" given as a meaning for the verb *aphiēmi*. Peter and Andrew "leave" their nets; James and John "leave" their father, Zebedee, with the workers in the boat.

I make this remark because quite often the commentaries slip in this meaning of "quitting," and this has led to outcomes and excesses that have troubled and wounded the consciences of many.

The Greek verb *aphiēmi* means "to leave," which is to say, to leave the other party free, to recognize his liberty or to return it to him. It is a verb of liberation to the other. Thus, in Matthew 19:14, Jesus requires that the little children be "left" to come freely to him. In the same way, in Mark 11:6, the owner of the donkey "left" the disciples to freely take the animal.

The verb meaning "to quit" is quite different, *kataleipō*: This is also a verb of liberty, but here for the subject of the verb. To quit (or desert) is to take one's own liberty in relation to others, as is the case with the man who "quits" his father and mother in order to marry (Matt 19:5); he needs his freedom if he is to establish a new home.

In the account of the disciples' calling, it is not at all said of them that they "quit" their connections in order to enjoy their liberty, but that they "left" the others, without imposing their choices on them, free in relation to Jesus' word.

This nuance, playing between the two verbs "to leave" and "to quit," bounces around in the passages that deal in a general way with becoming a disciple. "Whoever leaves, for my name's sake, his brothers or sisters, his father or mother, his wife or his children, his houses or lands, shall receive back a hundredfold and inherit eternal life" (Matt 19:29). It is the verb "leave" that is used and never the verb "quit," and the same can be seen in the parallel verses in Mark (10:29) and Luke (18:29), despite certain translations that mistakenly employ the verb "quit."

Never, in the Gospels, did Jesus ask a disciple to "quit" his family; he only asked that they "leave." The difference is important. The appeal given by Jesus is an invitation to leave others free in regard to the call, but not to let the weight of the vocation press on others, not to recruit them by force. To become a disciple means leaving those close to us free, renouncing any right over them, any power over them, any control, any hold, indeed any spiritual authority. It means leaving your loved ones free before God, leaving them to listen to God so that they hear him calling them. It is a question of liberty being recognized, respected, and in this there is a substantial act of love, an attitude of love.

How different this is to what is often preached, tilted towards the meaning "quit"; this does not emphasize the freedom of others but that of the disciple, who, in claiming his own liberty, breaks the ties of love, and wounds the love of others. Disciples have no need to claim their own liberty, nor to impose it, since they receives it from Christ.

If this is so, why has it been preached in the church that we must "quit" our loved ones, not "leave" them free? Where does it come from, this nonsense which has such grave consequences both for individual consciences and for families? In French[13] it comes from particular translations under the influence of the Latin Vulgate, which was the first to present this subversion of meaning. The error goes back to the fifth century and has been perpetuated even in the Protestant translations, though these are quite distant from the Latin; they have nevertheless been marked by it, even if only by the weight of tradition. This is why even in the translation of Segond we find "Whoever shall quit/desert for my names' sake his brothers or his sisters . . ." (Matt 19:29).

The hatred free[14] from hatred

With regard to the attitude Jesus required of his disciples when it came to their families, there is another very strong verse with a claim on our attention. "If anyone comes after me and does not hate his father, his mother, his spouse, his children, his brothers and sisters and even his own soul, he cannot be my disciple" (Luke 14:26).

How, Lord, can you require such a thing, you who always speak about love? You who have such a high view of love of one's neighbor, how can you speak of hate, and when it concerns the very closest of those close to us? Lord, I cannot get a hold of this. I don't understand it . . . !

Before we rebel, before we evade the difficulty or endeavor to sweeten it, before attempting the least commentary, it would be good

13. The reader may, like the translator, not have seen this explicitly in the English-speaking world, but may be able to think of situations influenced by similar ideas. One woman the translator was acquainted with accepted Christ; her friends immediately said, "you will have to quit [i.e. walk out on] Ian." She was smarter than that and said "no, he will follow me in"; he did, they got married, had children, became pastors. (Trans.)

14. French *exempte*—exempt from. (Trans.)

to begin with silence, a long, deep silence before God, perhaps even years of silence in nearness to Christ, years of growing intimacy with him, until the meaning of the word "hate" in his mouth takes on some clarity . . . because, whatever else, if Jesus requires that we hate our family, it must be because the word has a different meaning for him to the one we give it; and it must be that there is hatred other than what we are familiar with, a hatred of which our darkened hearts are ignorant, but a hatred that must correspond to a reality!

It is indeed a fact that this hatred exists, not, nevertheless, among men, but with God. He who is all-loving cried out one day that he felt hatred towards his dear ones, towards his own house: "I have forsaken my house. . . . I hate it . . . ," he said one day to his prophet Jeremiah (12:7–8); he was speaking of the nation of Israel, which was like a spouse to him, the well-beloved to whom he said elsewhere, "I love you with an eternal love" (Jer 31:3). What is the nature of this "hatred" that God experiences towards his well-beloved?

To understand the word "hate" on Jesus lips means understanding the meaning of the word as spoken by God.

In the seventh century of our era there was a man by the name of John, referred to today as John Climacus; he was, so to speak, buried with God, deep in the Sinai desert. After forty years of silence and divine intimacy, he began to write on life in God. In his chapter on discernment, we find from his pen an expression of extreme concision, a simple formula without any commentary, which shows the degree to which this intimacy with God brought discernment into this mystery of the hate required by Jesus, and experienced by God. It is, he says, "the hatred free from hatred" (26:14). A long and deep silence is again needed to take in this succinct and paradoxical saying and allow it to make its way inwards! How often truth is paradoxical . . . .

"Hatred free from hatred"; in our all too human mouths, the word "hatred" is charged with all our human sinfulness, our resentments, animosity, ill will; in short, with everything that has nothing to do with love . . . . In God, by contrast, hatred is quite different, imprinted with the purity of infinite love, totally stripped of all animosity, ill will, rancor . . . . Divine hatred is exempt from everything that is an issue of our spiritual maladies; it is hatred that is free from hatred!

"Hatred free of hatred"; yes, Lord, that's it! How wonderful; may you be blessed for this light from the desert, where your Holy Spirit blows . . . .

It required forty years passed in the crucible of the desert, in the crucible of God's love, before John Climacus was able to discern the infinite distance between human hatred and divine hatred, so like that between darkness and light. In God, hatred is a facet of his love; in man it is its negation.

When Jesus calls disciples to hate those of their own house, it is to be "the hatred free of hatred" that they are being invited, to the hatred totally purified by love. So, we need to understand clearly that we are absolutely incapable in ourselves of loving with this hatred, and so becoming disciples. God alone can enable us to live like this. He alone can fashion our hearts in the crucible of his love. He alone can transform our love and enable us to hate without hatred.

Lord my God, without you I can do nothing! In your infinite love, give me the grace to know how to fulfill your will, and enable me to become your disciple!

The church in gestation

On occasion, Jesus calls a disciple in isolation; this is the case with Levi for example, but here, with the first disciples, he calls them two by two. In each Gospel it is the same; there never was one first disciple. Two according to Matthew (4:20) and John (1:35–40), three according to Luke (5:10–11). Why so?

Because the church was just being born, and because the church is always made up of many. The church is a plural reality, given existence by Christ, and two is the minimum ecclesiastic plurality. We are never

34

alone in the church. An isolated disciple is always in communion with others; the greater the solitude, the more perceptible is this tie of fellowship; the solitaries of old were all witnesses to this.

We are viewing here the formation of the church, as Mark, no doubt, suggests with the verb he uses for "call" in verse 20, where Jesus "calls" James and John. The precise content of this call is not stated; the exact words addressed to the two disciples are passed over in silence, thereby drawing attention to the verb that summarizes it and draws out its deepest sense. He "called" them! From the verb "to call" (*kaleō*), the word for "church" (*ekklēsia*) is derived. The call of Christ is what constitutes the church. As he brings to birth these first vocations, Jesus brings the church to birth.

In this account, no disciple is set forth in distinction from the others. The church is the same; no disciple can be a disciple without the others; neither is any one greater than the others, even when, as in what follows, Peter has a function that makes him prominent. He is to be considered as a foundation, which is to say, that which humbly lies beneath the rest of the edifice.

Two by two

Fishing with a rod and line is something one can do on one's own, as Sunday fishermen know very well. By contrast, fishing with a net on the sea of Galilee in Christ's time could not be accomplished alone. The nets they used required the collaboration of at least two men; neither Peter nor Andrew could have worked alone, which is why they were together, the same as James and John. By calling the disciples two by two, Jesus makes us aware that no calling is to be lived alone, but always with others, in the church. A calling is not a personal affair, but always an ecclesiastic one. Certainly, each disciple is always called personally, and no one could respond in another's place, but there is always a church-wide perspective.

Matthew reflects this when he says that Peter and Andrew threw "a" net into the sea (4:18). It is by a pair that such a net is handled. This is a marvellous school of humility; no fisherman could attribute the success of his catch to himself alone, not when he is working with another.

When Jesus later sends out his disciples into the mission field, he sends them out two by two (Mark 6:7). Here again, the importance of the church setting of every mission is advanced, in every work the disciple undertakes. Two by two; this is one of the great secrets of the church, the secret of the Christian's humility and indeed of the perfect humility of Christ himself. Jesus sends the disciples two by two, but also made this very illuminating statement about the work effected by each pair of disciples: "Where there are two of you in my name, I am in the midst of you!" (Matt 18:20). This statement says a lot about the daily affairs of mission. Whenever two disciples work together, Christ is at work with them, mysteriously present, but in his great humility astonishingly hidden at times. So, as we learn to work in pairs in the church, we need to await the discovery of how Christ is collaborating with us. In fact, the *quorum*, so to speak, in the church is not two but three!

"Two by two"; in itself, this is a tremendous gift, the gift of a brother as well as the gift of Christ mysteriously present. The grace of Christ's mysterious presence is a wonderful gift, but the gift of a brother or sister is also wonderful in moments of discouragement, temptation, spiritual struggle.

"Two by two"; when Jesus calls the first disciples, the intent is not to turn them towards each other, but that they follow together after him, that he may lead them to others and to the Father. Even between two disciples, the relationship takes place through Christ, and this also is the mystery of the church. There is no turning in on oneself, nor is there a turning to another within a pair, but always a looking out, an opening onto a third; more than just a one-on-one encounter.

This also helps us better understand the mystery of God. In God, indeed, in the Trinity, there is no face to face between just two persons. Communion between the Father and the Son always includes communion with the Holy Spirit, and still more than that; this communion of the three persons of the Trinity is open to humanity. The love of the Trinity is in no way turned inward; it is wonderfully open to us.

Dorothea of Gaza proposes a very beautiful image to describe the church. He compares it to a wheel, the hub of which is Christ and of which we are the spokes. The image depicts how it is in approaching Christ that we approach each other; otherwise it is impossible, despite all our efforts. This is profound truth! It is indeed in approaching Christ that we truly draw near to others. In ecumenical dialogue, today, this is very important. We should not seek first to get close to one another, but rather make every effort, firstly, each one, to draw near to God; it's then that rapprochement between churches can become evident.

The church, then, has its beginning in this small but plural number, but also with the fact that the plurality has no place for anonymity. Each disciple, indeed, has a name—Peter, Andrew, James, John . . . a name, which is to say a recognized identity, respected and honored. God calls us by name and this is how he brings us to being. It is striking to see how there were disciples also to be found around John the Baptist, but by contrast, that their names are not recorded (Matt 11:2), as if to say that the particularity of the church is that each person has a name, their true identity. The rich young man who Jesus invited to become a disciple, but who declined the offer, has no name! He brushed shoulders with and then walked right past the true life.

Follow me

The first word addressed by Jesus to Peter was an invitation to follow him. The last word from Jesus to Peter, in John's Gospel was the same, "Follow me!" (John 21:22). There is more matter here to consider. It is good to tell ourselves that it will doubtless be the same for each of us. "Follow me"; this is the first word Jesus speaks to us, an invitation that can always be renewed, to the very end!

These great appeals which bracket Peter's story bring a further deepening to the meaning of the call. For Peter, the final "follow me" resounds after the episode of his denial as an implicit declaration of forgiveness, and this surely applies to us as well with our denials! But there is more yet.

At the close of the Gospel, when Jesus says "follow me!" it is at the moment when he is about to disappear from the sight of the disciples. Following Jesus in Galilee after first being called was to have him before their eyes; but to follow him when he was absent, what would that mean? The question is important because it certainly applies to us. When Jesus calls us today we cannot see him. How then are we to follow him without being able to march concretely, physically, behind him? Our situation today is not that of Peter at the outset of the Gospel, but his at its close. How can we follow the one who, since his ascension, is absent?

The context of the final encounter between Jesus and Peter makes it quite apparent that it was also the disciple's place to follow Jesus in death (21:19). It is a fact that the cross is unavoidable in the life of every disciple. Following Christ also means carrying his cross! This is not all though. When Jesus invites Peter to follow him he is speaking as the Resurrected One. This means following the Living One, beyond the cross. What can the invitation to follow the Resurrected Christ mean?

A paradox is evident at the moment the Resurrected Christ prepares to ascend to heaven, since he affirms to his disciples that he will be vividly present to them. "I am with you, even unto the end of the world," he says to them at the end of the Gospel (Matt 28:20).

"I am with you," he says as he makes himself absent, or, rather, unseen. After the ascension, Christ would never be absent to the disciples, but at the same time, neither would he be present! Effectively his absence is necessary to allow of his presence. The whole of the farewell discourse (John 14 to 16) seeks to elucidate this paradox. I must go away so that I can be all the more present to you, Christ explains. No longer *with* you, as I have been until now, but *in* you as I have never yet been.

These sayings of Jesus bring the understanding that Christ passes from one mode of presence to another, and that this passage is achieved by his absence. Jesus is not simply with us but in us, in an unseen form but none the less real.

How are we to follow one who is so mysteriously both present and absent?

The paradox of love

The paradox of the presence/absence of Christ finds its resolution in love, which is not so surprising, since Jesus is the very incarnation of the paradox of love. Following him consists in loving as he himself loves.

True love is made up of both absence and presence, distance and proximity, in a balance that is difficult for us to achieve. Love is able both to keep its distance so as not to squash the other, not to invade and suffocate. It is not possessive and so keeps a distance. Modern psychology has well underlined the ravages wrought by love that is possessive, invasive, and suffocating.

This same modern psychology has also underlined how significant are the ravages wrought by a love that is too distant, too absent, experienced as abandonment.

Perfect love avoids both pitfalls and is able to make itself neither too present nor too absent. The love of the Risen Christ for his disciples, like that of God for his children, is so extraordinarily present as to be *in* the disciples, without ever being invasive; and so extraordinarily apart, respecting our liberty, at a distance which allows the disciple to blossom.

The love of the Trinity is this perfect love. The Father loves the Son, but maintaining a distinct distance, which the Gospels note as they record the words addressed by the Father to the Son. Is he too distant? That is not at all the experience of Christ, who makes this statement denoting an incomparable presence: "The Father is in me, and I am in the Father" (John 14:10).

Nevertheless, on the cross, for the space of a moment only, the Son believes himself to have been abandoned: "My God, my God, why have you forsaken me?" He says this, however, and experiences it in such proximity of prayer that it is immediately linked to another prayer of great intimacy: "Father, into your hands I commit my spirit."

The trinitarian love that fills Christ is the love he experiences with us: "as the Father has loved me, so have I loved you" (John 15:9).

To follow Christ is to follow on the same path, no longer the paths of Galilee, but the path of perfect love, where he himself stands unseen, wonderfully apart and wonderfully present.

— CHAPTER 2 —

Come unto Me

BECOMING A DISCIPLE IS not something that happens in an instant, in a few hours, or even a few days; this is not because of any incompetence in the master but rather because of the darkness of our spirits, the resistance of our hearts, the incoherence of our desires, the burdens of our human existence, and our spiritual weakness . . . . It is a long work of apprenticeship. After the call to discipleship, how does the disciple's formation take place in the master's presence?

The word for "disciple" in Greek, *mathētēs*, derives from a verb *manthanō*, which means "to learn." The verb appears rarely in the Gospels, but it is found once in Jesus' mouth in the expression "learn of me." The single use of this expression merits our full attention. The text where it is found clearly shows Jesus' hearers to be disciples or future disciples, and Jesus as the master who proposes to train[1] them.

"Learn of me." We can't get away from this proposal of Jesus if we are to understand how he sees the instruction of his disciples, how we are to become disciples.

> "*Come unto me all you who are weary and heavy laden and I will give you rest. Take my yoke upon you and learn of me because I am meek and lowly of heart, and you will find rest for your souls; for my yoke is easy and my burden is light.*" (Matt 11:28–30)

---

1. The French is *former*, literally "to form"; this fits well with the idea of "spiritual formation," but in so far as a master "trains" an apprentice, that has been the preferred translation here. (Trans.)

The day he called them, Jesus said to his disciples, "Come, follow me"; now he employs a slightly different phrase, "Come *unto* me," giving his words a gentle twist, conveying the meaning of a much greater proximity. He who was always on the move, unceasingly in motion, seems now to wish to stop, to sit down perhaps, to observe a pause, time at least for some instruction . . . "Come unto me."

This pause seems all the more necessary in that Jesus is speaking to those who are tired and in need of time out: "Come to me, all you who are weary and heavily burdened and I will give you some repose." Christ's teaching is to take place in a moment of respite, in the midst of the whirlwind, in the trials of life. Blessed disciples, who have to do with a master who watches over them, attentive to their weariness!

An amazing rabbi . . .

When he says "learn of me," Jesus is presenting himself as a true master, a true rabbi in the nomenclature of the time, but a rabbi who greatly intrigued his contemporaries because of the amazing difference between him and other rabbis. In fact, in a most singular way, Jesus was a man whom many termed "rabbi," which is to say "my master," but who nevertheless had not himself been taught by any other rabbi; and you don't become a rabbi without first having been a disciple. In Jesus' case, no one knew who his rabbi was—who had been his instructor?

This question did not fail of being asked, and John's Gospel has an echo of it when it reports the remarks made in the temple in Jerusalem one day; certain Jews observed him teaching in this high place, and said, "How does this man know the Scriptures, never having been taught?" (John 7:15). From what these Jews said we note the verb "to teach," from which is derived the word for "disciple," so what they said comes to this: "how does he know the Scriptures, never having been a disciple?"

Jesus does not evade the question, but gives an unequivocal answer: "My teaching is not my own, but his who sent me." No, Jesus was not self-taught, and had received his teaching from someone; but it is important from whom, from "he who sent me," which comes to saying, from God himself! This is a new source of astonishment; no rabbi had ever been directly trained by God! God indeed is the source of all teaching, but always through a human intermediary. This was a unique rabbi, with no resemblance to any other! What was he? A proud rascal, a blaspheming charlatan, or a messenger from God, sent from the Father as he proposed . . . ? To join his school, respond to his call, is a real act of faith . . . . "Come unto me! Enrol in my school . . . !"

. . . and amazing disciples

When it comes to matters for astonishment, we have not finished yet! In fact, Jesus will surprise us again by forbidding his disciples to let themselves ever be called "rabbi." Once trained, instead of themselves becoming rabbis, Jesus' disciples were not to think of themselves as masters. John the Baptist had disciples (John 1:35; Luke 7:18–24) and he was referred to as "rabbi" (John 3:26). Among the Pharisees, their rabbis also had disciples (Luke 5:33), but the disciples of Jesus were not future masters: "But you," Jesus said to them, "you are not to be called Rabbi, because you have one master alone, and you are all brothers" (Matt 23:8).

Nevertheless, after the resurrection, Jesus sends his disciples to teach, and then prescribes that they "make disciples" (Matt 28:19). In fact, there were to be teachers in the church (Acts 13:1; 1 Cor 12:28), but the disciples they trained were not to be their disciples. Neither Matthew, nor Mark, Luke, John, Paul, Peter, nor James, nor any other disciple was to have disciples! Nobody in the church is a disciple of anyone other than Jesus. Disciples trained up by the disciples were always considered "disciples of the Lord" (Acts 9:1).

This then, in contrast to Judaism, was the arrangement in the church, according to the will of the Lord; one person alone has the standing of master, Christ. Each disciple is a disciple of Christ alone, and of no one else.

After a time of formation alongside Jesus, the disciples in their turn would be sent out to teach, to make new disciples. They would then be called "apostles," that is "sent ones." This is an aspect of the disciples' lives we need to guard in our spirits because it gives a particular meaning and perspective to their formative period; I will not discuss this here, in order to focus on the disciple's time of apprenticeship by Jesus' side, but we must realize that there is a consequence, an enlargement, an apostolate, a mission. "To be an apostle" might be the subject of a further retreat.

Take my yoke

Between "come to me" and "learn of me" Jesus states another instruction, addressed to the same listeners, and which we need to examine now since it describes the condition under which the proposed teaching is to unfold: "take my yoke."

We go from one surprise to the next; this expression is a metaphor no doubt, but a particularly surprising one.

Jesus proposed teaching is not to take place behind the desks of a school but under a yoke! It is not at a theoretical level, but is to immediately entail the conditions of practical labor; the yoke is an instrument of work, of work indeed that is wearing and exhausting! This is a strange rabbi, with strange methods!

Neither is Jesus' proposed instruction to be given in some holy place; not in the annex of a synagogue, nor on the grounds of the temple in Jerusalem, where such servile labor was formally forbidden. It was to be given in the places where a yoke is borne, that is, somewhere profane; not on the Sabbath, but during the course of daily life since yokes were proscribed on the Sabbath and feast days, just as was any and all labor. This was a decidedly strange rabbi!

Free or slaves?

At Jesus' time, in the context of Roman culture, a yoke would evoke the image of submission to a conqueror. After a war, in fact, the vanquished would "pass under the yoke," stooping beneath a bar termed "the yoke," in a sign of submission and servitude. That is not, however, what is in view here. Jesus does not say "come under my yoke" but "carry my yoke," clearly putting this into the realm of work, not war.

Biblically, bearing a yoke denotes the most tiring work, most often carried out by a stranger in a context of enslavement. Thus it was that Israel bore the yoke of Egypt (Lev 26:13), of Assyria (Isa 14:25), of Babylon (Jer 28:2), and then of all the peoples who became their masters. Again, that is not what is in view here; Jesus is not presenting himself as a dominator; he is not imposing his yoke but proposing it! He does not subjugate, he invites: "Come unto me, take my yoke." The invitation is addressed to the free, those who have entire liberty to respond, to accept or refuse.

If we wish to find a precedent in the Old Testament there is one clearly there, also in the fashion of an invitation to take on a yoke, and also for the training of disciples, not as an imposition on slaves. Before Jesus, it was the Wisdom of God giving the invitation to whoever would heed it: "Come to me, those who are without instruction, enrol in my school, put your neck under the yoke and your soul will receive instruction" (Sir 51:23, 26).[2] The similarity of expression here is striking. Jesus is operating within the context of wisdom, not that of an invading warrior; he even presents himself as the Wisdom of God in person! Anyone who wishes to be wise has only to draw near to him

2. In some versions of this text from Ecclesiasticus (or Sirach) the verses are 31 and 34. (Trans.)

and take on his yoke. The image of the yoke is that of work undertaken freely in order to learn the wisdom of God, not the work of a slave for the profit of a tyrant of oppressor.

Of what type of work are we to think? Of all work done in the name of Christ. Whether the work is that of a deacon, work with the handicapped, the elderly, with refugees, with the unemployed, or an internal work, a work on oneself, everything done under the yoke of Christ, under his authority, in the course of daily life, every work is a place of concrete apprenticeship in which the disciple is formed.

Come unto me, all you who are weary and heavy laden

The picture of the yoke for work done in the daily reality of life is interesting, but it must be recognized that when we think about who Jesus is speaking to, "you, the weary and heavy laden," it seems incongruous and even misplaced, for which read unrealistic! To propose a yoke, which is an extra burden, to those who are already weighed down and exhausted, is rather hard, a little sadistic! Such an invitation seems shocking, unacceptable!

What are you saying, Lord? Life is tough enough as it is; each day's load is hard enough to bear. How can you propose something that will be an extra weight? Is this the wisdom of God . . . ?

I understand the complaint uttered in the twelfth century by Guillaume de Saint Thierry, who, like so many other Christians, felt that being a disciple was a burden too great to bear, too heavy a weight, and that to be a Christian is more wearisome than not to be one.

> You have deceived me, Lord, and I allowed myself to be fooled. You were too strong and swept me away. I heard your voice when you said, "Come to me you are troubled and burdened and I will relieve you!" I came to you; I have believed your word. But in what way have you given me relief? I was

untroubled, but now I am distressed, so heavily that I suc-
cumb. I was not overburdened, but now I bow beneath the
weight. You said, nevertheless, "My yoke is sweet and my
burden is light." Where is this sweetness? Where is the light-
ness? I cannot cope under this yoke, I fall beneath the load. I
looked despairingly for a comforter, but no one came to my
aid! I looked, but there was no one to help. What am I to do,
Lord? Have pity on me, for I am sick . . . ![3]

The pain is real, but there is a terrible misunderstanding here;
Jesus' invitation is truly a wonderful statement about the way of the
good news of the kingdom. The yoke is an incomparable grace, formed
out of a wonderful love. We must take time to listen to Christ.

The grace of the yoke

The particularity of a yoke is that it is not borne alone, but by a pair.
Other instruments are used if an animal is to work alone, but the property of the yoke is that it is placed on two necks, which are thus joined
by it; and if not, it is not a yoke. In proposing a yoke, Jesus is not wishing to overwhelm one who suffers and can manage no more, but, on
the contrary, wishes to share the burden by bringing in another person.
Proposing a yoke to somebody means lightening the burden by half. It
is not to altogether remove it, to be sure, but is nonetheless an immense
relief, a true act of grace.

Jesus does not present himself as being about to remove every difficulty from life, making every weight disappear. It would be wrong to
make a disciple believe that there will be no load, no more problems or
difficulties, no reverses, no checks or temptations, no more burden . . . .
Jesus is not opening a road to dreamland, to a fantasy world. He brings
us face to face with the reality of life while proposing an easing, a relief.

3. *Méditation et prières* [Meditations and prayers] (Paris: O.E.I.L., 1985), 215.

Further to this, the proposal of the yoke will cause all solitude to be gone. The difficulty of life, its hardship, also lies in having to face it alone and carry the burden alone. The proposed yoke brings an end to solitude. Henceforth, we will not be alone, but will have another to help bear whatever the weight is within our lives; what good news! You will have observed, reader friend, that the tiring nature of a task accomplished alone disappears almost entirely when the same job is shared with someone else. It is a relief, and sometimes even a joy, to share the weight of a task with another. The presence of another is a gift of grace.

"You will find rest for your soul." When we discover that the rest Jesus announces has to do with the soul, and that the weariness of those Jesus invites has also to do with the soul, then Jesus' remarks open up marvellous new horizons. The weariness of trials, cares, checks, and sins that have to be borne is all the worse in that it affects the soul, the deepest place of our being.

As we contemplate these marvellous prospects, one further question arises; who is this other who will be by our side under the yoke Jesus proposes? Who is that will be able to carry the burden of life with me, the burden that crushes the soul? Jesus does not specify clearly, but as we look a little more closely, what exactly does he mean to say when he says "take *my* yoke"?

Take *my* yoke upon you

A frequent comment with regard to the yoke has been to make Christ the one who drives the team after imposing his yoke, like a plowman driving his beasts, a comment that never explains who might be found alongside us, sharing the yoke. The picture is falsified in this way; a yoke requires two people to carry it. The question cannot be avoided; who will bear the yoke with us?

"Come unto me," Jesus starts by saying before he speaks of his yoke. "Come unto me" means, come alongside me . . . . I trust that makes things clear; the other one, by our side, is none other than Jesus himself! His yoke is truly his, his yoke, the yoke he places on my shoulders at the same time as it lies on his, joining himself to me and thus sharing my pains, my burdens, my weights, everything that is heaped upon me . . . . How wonderful!

What good news this is! But also, what love and humility on Jesus' part, inviting us to draw near to him so that he can be beside us and carry with us the burden of our daily life! How wonderful that this master should come alongside his disciple, at the same level, to team up with him for the daily round! What a lightening of the load for the disciple, what relief! What a joy to see the pain of solitude gone in exchange for such extraordinary accompaniment, step by step through life! Indeed it is no lie when he says that his yoke is sweet and his burden light!

To tell the truth, Lord, I really cannot see who, other than you, would be able to bear the weight of my soul with me! But I would never have dared ask this! How wonderful you are to propose this in your great humility and unequalled love!

"Come unto me, take my yoke upon you, all you who are worn and weighed down, and I will give you rest"; what a magnificent invitation! Not only is this to be received with gratitude, but it also needs to be passed on to all those who are likewise weary and heavily laden; you too may come to Christ! He awaits you with his yoke, and proposes to bear with you the weight of your life.

A long apprenticeship

This is how, beneath his yoke, we learn to become disciples of the one who humbly takes his place beside us. It is wonderful, but the apprenticeship is also lengthy. To bear a yoke is not something learnt in a morning. For anyone who has never done this, it is not easy to become accustomed to the new way of life, to this new way of working.

Why, though, would we not learn it if it is the condition for benefiting from the unceasing nearness of Christ? We could hardly be closer than under the same yoke, and this will continue as long as the yoke binds us; it is each step of the way, and even during any pause to catch breath before we go on together.

Learning to be a disciple, learning to bear the yoke, means learning to go at the rhythm and pace of the one beside you. For us this is no small matter; learning to match our pace with that of Christ. This is the business of a lifetime!

Learning to bear a yoke means learning to harmonize your efforts with those of your partner. Learning to live like this beside Christ on a daily basis is, again, a lifetime's endeavor . . . .

Learning to bear a yoke means learning to march in the same furrow, under the direction of the same pilot. Who then is the director? Who is there that Christ would obey other than his Father? To live like this with Christ, in the same obedience to God, is also the business of a lifetime . . . .

How demanding, but again, what grace, since, under a yoke, each adapts to the pace of the other, to the other's rhythm and effort; this also means that Christ, so humble and loving as to be by our side, is still more humble and loving in exerting himself to adapt to our pace, to our rhythm, to cheer us when he sees us weak, to compensate for our thousand failings . . . . What a wonderful companion he truly is, acting like this in his grace, always encouraging lest we resign our commission, pull back or despair . . . . Once allied under the same yoke, Christ never lets go, never defaults! Faithfully, he stays to the end, cost what it may, at the price of his life if need be . . . . What joy!

Another peculiarity of the yoke is that it causes two beasts to go forward together without being able to see each other. They are very, very close, always alongside each other, feeling each other, touching each other, but not seeing each other! There is a good picture here of how very close our partner is, though remaining unseen . . . . The more compelling and demanding the work, the more silent the team; again this is a reality of faith. Christ is silent by our side, and his silence results from his total investment and application to our common employment. This silence is very wonderful, that of Christ beside us!

If the disciple and the master are engaged in a common work under the same yoke, this doesn't mean there is a perfect equality between us. Both are totally implicated in the work, but the master is still the master, teaching the disciple to march under the yoke, and the disciple is still the disciple, learning from his master how to behave under the yoke.

When we wish to teach a young animal, still wild and inexperienced, to bear the yoke, he is teamed up with an older animal, already experienced and docile. This is the best type of apprenticeship! The same for us, as you will have understood!

To march together under a yoke is a wonderful school of mutual trust, of attention to the other, and mutual obedience to the pilot. All this is taught us in tandem with Christ, knowing that our confidence in Christ is echoed by the confidence of Christ in us. Indeed, Christ also places confidence in his disciple when he marches alongside him or her, and this confidence is such a force that the burden seems lighter.

"My yoke is easy"

In this picture, to what does the yoke, described as easy,[4] correspond?

A yoke is attached to the animals with ties and straps that bind them in tightly, and in this way they are also bound to each other. What tie is there to bind us to Christ other than that of love? Ancient commentators on the picture are unanimous; the yoke that unites us with Christ is love; the sweetness of his yoke is the sweetness of his love. This is why the burden becomes light; the love of Christ, which unites us to him, makes every burden light.

4. French *doux*, soft, smooth, sweet. (Trans.)

Earlier I made reference to the complaint of Guillaume de Saint Thierry, addressed to Christ in a prayer of great sincerity. Here is the response he received from the Lord:

> I have not deceived you, my son, but have led you gently to this point. You are murmuring because I do not bring relief, but if I had not in fact given you the relief you think you lack, you would have already succumbed! You groan under my yoke, and grow tired of my burden, but love gives sweetness to my yoke and lightness to my burden. You are incapable of bearing my burden and my yoke alone, but if love unites with you to bear them, to your huge astonishment you will immediately taste of their sweetness.

Not only is the sweetness of the yoke that of love, but Christ presented himself to Guillaume as the personification of love, the love that bore the yoke with him. Nevertheless, in the midst of his suffering, Guillaume did not immediately understand; he believed that the love in question was to be his own, then only later that it was the Lord's. This is how he continued his prayer:

> Lord, this is exactly what I've been telling you; I have done all that I could. Everything that seems to be in my power I have put to your service. If I could have had love, I would long since have been perfect. If you don't give it to me, I cannot have it. How little capable I am of anything, as you well know and you see! Relieve me of this misery however you please, but give me this love in its fullness and perfection! And as long as I have not this love, will you help me to bear my pain?

Then Guillaume understood this wonderful reply from the Lord: "It is I who have borne your pain all along, and I will continue to bear it!" If Christ so bears the pain that Guillaume bore too, it must indeed be that they bear it together under the same yoke!

To take up his cross _____

The image of the yoke proposed to the disciples is very close to another also proposed by Jesus to anyone who wishes to become his disciple: "Whoever would come after me, let him deny himself, let him take up his cross and follow me"(Matt 16:24).The cross, in the gospel message, is as unavoidable as the yoke for a disciple. In both cases, the disciples' place is to "take up," and exactly the same Greek verb is employed; to take up the cross and to take up the yoke.

However, the first difference between the yoke and the cross is in the possessives that qualify them, *my* yoke and *your* cross. The second is that a yoke is borne by two whereas the cross is carried alone, which indeed is a part of the torture, the fact that, right to the end, it is borne alone. Do we therefore need to renounce the wonderful companion-ship of Christ when it comes to the cross? Or is it that first we bear the yoke with him, and then the cross alone.

It is striking to note that the invitation to take up the cross is found in each of Matthew (16:24), Mark (8:34), and Luke (9:23), and that the same three Evangelists agree in saying that Jesus did not him-self succeed in carrying his own cross! He didn't manage it! He quit along the way . . . .

How, Lord, can this be? Are you asking of me something at which you failed? Never, Lord, have you required a disciple to do more than you did! Do you now wish me to carry my cross, when you did not bear your own . . . ?

At the very moment Jesus gave way under the weight, the Roman authority took pity; they commandeered one Simon of Cyrene to carry his cross.[5] This was an exceptional mercy to find in the executioners. Luke specifies that Simon was stood "behind Jesus" as he carried the cross with him (23:26); they bore it together.

---

5. For a full treatment of this episode see the author's *The Silence of God during the Passion*. (Trans.)

My child, says Christ, I was blessed with a gift. When I fell beneath my cross, I sensed someone come to my aid. I felt behind me the silence of his presence, the silence of his exertions. I experienced the wonderful relief of unexpected help. I had not asked anything, but nevertheless was blessed by an unbelievable mercy, that of my pitiless executioners. Do you believe, my child, that I don't know what it is to give way beneath a cross, to be crushed, overwhelmed and to quit? Do you believe my pity is less than that of a tyrant, and that I will not be gracious to you . . . ?

Let us be silent, reader friend, and bear our cross! The faithful disciples of Christ who have borne their cross are unanimous in their testimony: at the moment the weight becomes too heavy and even unbearable, at the moment we fall, there, suddenly, the burden is made lighter, an unexpected presence is manifest in the silence of our effort. Someone is there behind us, in the same place as Simon of Cyrene. When the moment comes, you will surely recognize who it is behind you, in silence, bearing your cross with you . . . . You will recognize him by the sound of his tread, the same sound you heard beside you, beneath the yoke . . . .

What does he wish us to learn from him?

Let us return to the picture of the yoke, the day-by-day walk with Christ, to this school proposed to us to make us disciples. What are we going to learn from Christ? He himself provides the answer: "Learn of me, for I am gentle and lowly of heart."

Here are two virtues of Christ, gentleness and humility; two virtues among all those that are his that he wishes to teach us, that we may make them our own. Why would he advance these two in particular? Quite simply, it seems to me, because these two virtues are *par excellence* those that are most indispensable when it comes to bearing a yoke if this instrument of work is not to become an instrument of torture. The more gentle and humble the animal, the easier and lighter becomes the yoke, and also the easier and lighter it becomes on the shoulders of its partner. Gentleness and lowliness, two essential qualities for accompanying Christ.

To be beneath the yoke with Christ is to discover how gentle and lowly he is; it means experiencing this gentleness and lowliness, experiencing it concretely, and as its primary beneficiary. The more we walk by faith in the daily round of life, the more we appreciate the degree to which the Lord is gentle and lowly towards us, the extent of the blessing in having such a master by our side; and the more we exert ourselves to become likewise gentle and lowly, and step forward in greater harmony with him.

John Cassian noted that only the gentle and humble really know how to love. He was certainly right; the teaching of taking on the yoke on a daily basis confirms this.

A stiff neck

The opposite, the lack of gentleness and humility, is to have a "stiff neck," and this is particularly unsuitable for yoke bearing. To have a stiff neck is an expression frequently employed in the Old Testament to describe the prideful non-submission of Israel to God, their refusal to be taught by God.

The first time the expression is used it is full of humor on God's part. Its first occurrence, in fact, is on God's lips at the moment he informs Moses that the people have fashioned a golden calf (Exod 32:9). According to Israel, this calf represented the image of God who had brought them up out of Egypt. A calf made of the most precious of metals—that's the way to honor God! For God however, the calf is nothing but a caricature, but not of him, but of the people, because at the end of the day Israel's neck was as stiff as any golden calf! An untamed and proud people, upon whom no yoke can be laid; that is what we are in truth!

Gentleness

Under a yoke, gentleness is an immense blessing to one's teammate, since it prevents many sufferings. The slightest abrupt movement can cause the yoke to bounce, and this can prove most painful; any sudden turn or halt hurts the other as well as oneself; the yoke hurts both necks. Happily for us, Christ is wonderfully gentle and we benefit at every moment from this gentleness. It is beneath this yoke, as we walk with him day by day, that we discover and prove his gentleness, not in spiritual books or theological discourses. Apprenticeship in the gentleness of Christ takes place in apprenticeship at his side in life.

What would Christ in his gentleness teach us if not to become gentle ourselves in his image, through association with him? If, by his gentleness, Christ frees us from many sufferings, we can also spare ourselves much suffering by ourselves becoming gentle. In fact, the least of our impetuosities, our refusals, our harsh reactions, all wound both us and Christ. These wounds we inflict on ourselves through our lack of gentleness are not a punishment inflicted by the driver of the team, nor indeed by Christ; they are the fruit of our own attitude, stemming from our lack of gentleness, our rebellions, our insubmission. We do ill to ourselves by not submitting, by our disobedience to God. This is one aspect of suffering that it is good to be aware of. Rather than accuse God of punishing us, we should recognize that through our lack of submission to God we hurt ourselves.

Meekness

The Greek word translated as "gentle" (*praus*) also means "tamed" or "broken in" when speaking of an animal, or we might say "docile."[6] The two different senses of the Greek word correspond to two similar sounding words in romance languages, as in the Latin, *dolcis* and *docilis*; we will stay with the Greek and consider the two meanings together in the one word.

Beneath a yoke, the principal beneficiary of gentleness is the team mate, whereas docility is above all appreciated by the driver, the pilot, which is to say, where we are concerned, God.

Just as Christ is gentle towards us, in the same way he is meek towards his Father, obedient to his word, entirely submitted to his commandments and his will. "Father, not my will, but yours be done" (Luke 22:42).

Obedience nowadays does not always get a good press, even in the church, with its connotation for us of servility and debasement. The obedience that we find in Jesus towards his Father has nothing servile about it, but is an obedience full of love, a voluntary submission, free and dictated by love alone. It is indeed the opposite of a stiff neck.

What Christ is looking for in us, our docility towards his Father's word and will, towards his slightest desire, we cannot find simply in books, but it must be in the course of daily life as we apply ourselves to life beside him. The meekness the Gospels speak of is something we assimilate as we go about living under its sway, in company with Christ. It is the schooling of the yoke that teaches us to become obedient to God. We learn true obedience from Christ.

Meekness towards God is a matter of abandonment; not abandonment of what we have, but of what we are. It is less a matter of abandoning some particular thing than of abandoning ourselves to God, abandoning ourselves in love. Abandonment of self to the Father

6. The French reads *docile*; meek has been preferred in translation as more traditional in English. (Trans.)

takes form in confident and loving obedience alongside Christ, Christ who, in his meekness, himself perfectly embodies it. This again is the business of a lifetime . . . .

Gentleness and meekness are not separate; there is just one word in Greek, and with good reason! If you wish to know, reader friend, the full measure of what the fathers have passed down to us, and wish to make proof of your wisdom by being gentle with your brothers, then know that it is in being meek towards God that you can become truly gentle with others. How true this is! What the fathers say on this, they learned from Christ as they walked with him beneath the same yoke.

What is the source of our lack of meekness towards God? Our pride, assuredly! From our pretentious desire to direct ourselves, from wishing to ignore the pilot, from supposing we know better than him what is best for us to do! Pride makes us insubmissive towards God and harsh towards our brothers.

Pride is so perfidious and subtle that it makes us believe we can love God without obeying him. To love God while allowing ourselves to disobey him, even with regard to just one of his instructions, means falling into the trap, the illusion secretly offered by pride.

If in this way pride is the source of our indocility, then we can understand why Jesus is led to speak of humility as well as gentleness. He does this, not to set forward his own humility (which would be an indication of pride), but to enable us to understand quite simply the source of his gentleness, what its origins are; he makes this very clear, very plain, teaching us and showing us the true way of meekness towards God.

Humility of heart

To be humble is one thing, but to be lowly or humble of heart is something else, infinitely more extraordinary. The fathers[7] made careful note

7. The author is here using the term in a wider, non-technical sense, to indicate

of the way there are, in reality, many degrees of humility. According to the analysis of Nicetas Stethatos, for example, (twelfth century), first of all there is humility of speech; this is the first step of humility, the easiest, the most accessible for whoever wishes to take pains over it, the help of God being understood here, since without God any effort at humility will only produce pride. By dint of spiritual struggle, human determination, and divine aid, humility of speech is easily enough achieved.

The second step, less frequent, less accessible, and more difficult, is humility of comportment. One might indeed be humble in one's speech, without yet being humble in attitude. It is quite possible to be humble in discourse and proud in conduct; this is to be a hypocrite and reveals the way pride can continue to lie concealed behind humble words. To achieve humility in comportment is the fruit of extended spiritual struggle at every moment, requiring unremitting efforts on oneself and total collaboration with the grace of God.

The third step of humility is properly speaking inaccessible to humans, and is the pure grace of God; this is humility of heart. Where there is a ditch between humility of speech and humility of comportment, there is a chasm between this last and humility of heart! No one amongst humanity has been able to cross this chasm except Christ and those he has made like himself by his grace. Humility of heart is, in the first place, the humility of God himself, of the Father, of the Son, and of the Holy Spirit.

Beneath the yoke, as we walk step by step alongside the Lord, the Holy Spirit enables us to discover little by little the extreme humility of Christ, the humility that lies deep in his heart. It is also wonderful to be able to discover at the same time, little by little, in the Gospel accounts, how great this humility is. It is wonderful because at the same time there is also revealed the deep humility of the Father and of the Holy Spirit. Humility of heart is the full depth of the mystery of divine love.

---

spiritual leaders in the historic church. (Trans.)

To discover, little by little, beneath the yoke, how Christ is gentle and lowly of heart immerses our own heart deep in contemplative silence. Discovering the heart humility of Christ is to penetrate into the mystery of his heart, into the inaccessible depths of his heart . . . . This surely touches on the miraculous! Who indeed can sound the depths of Christ's heart except for the one who "knows the depths of God" (1 Cor 2:10), that is, the Holy Spirit? To discover, beneath the yoke, little by little, Christ's lowliness of heart is to be led by the Holy Spirit, fashioned slowly by him, transformed little by little. Only a transformed outlook, a transformed heart, can enter the mystery of Christ's heart and follow him on the road of humility.

This Gospel passage is unique in being the only one in the whole Bible to speak of Jesus' heart. No one other than Jesus spoke of his heart. The Father alone knows it, and only the Spirit can reveal it to us, since he alone can get to the very bottom of our pride, the pride that renders us blind and deaf to this subject.

Walking beneath the yoke then, in the final reckoning, is to be indwelt by the Holy Spirit, alongside the Son, under the direction of the Father. This step by step walk in the mystery of the Trinity proceeds in silence and wonderment . . . .

Synergy

"Without me you can do nothing"; these words of Christ reported in John's Gospel (15:5) fit in perfectly with the picture of the yoke. It is so very true that without a teammate alongside you in the same yoke, it is quite clearly impossible to do anything whatsoever.

The picture of the yoke is without doubt the best way of speaking about synergy, that is, the collaboration of effort, which results in the pooling of energy to one end. When two beasts are beneath one yoke, what becomes evident is not the relative strength of each but the strength of the two together, not the work effectuated by either individually, but that of the two together.

When he invites us to take up his yoke, Christ is inviting us to a life of synergy with him, a life in which it is no longer possible for us to know what comes from him and what from us. Beneath this yoke of love and humility, no one is keeping accounts, but each humbly attributes all that is essential to the other.

Beneath the yoke, there no longer exists any work we can call our own, any personal work, but instead the work is common to both. It is the only school where it is not possible to learn individualism! The only school where the first person singular gives place to the first person plural, such that the disciple will never be able to say, "look what I did," but only, "look what we've done, the two of us together . . . ." Then, in wonderment before this fact, we will be humbly silent about our part, unceasingly giving glory to the Lord.

Looking at the matter still more closely, the work performed by a team is not the work of the animals so much as that of the pilot who directs the team, since without him nothing is possible. The beasts, left to themselves, would be incapable of carrying out their task. It is the pilot who brings it all to realization by the way he sets about the work and causes it to happen. When a job is well done, it is not the team which is admired and glorified but the one who directs it with his expert hand, by the exercise of his skill.

Perfect synergy lies in common obedience to the director of the team, in harmony, in full complicity with him. Then fatigue is not a factor; it even disappears, the yoke is so sweet and the burden so light.

Continuing synergy

Not only do we find that the time of the disciples' formation is a time of learning to work together with Jesus, alongside him, under the same yoke, but we also discover in the Gospel that the same synergistic working together continues when the disciples cease to be disciples properly speaking, and become apostles, sent out on a mission.

One might think that the yoke is a very suitable way to describe the period of apprenticeship, the three years the twelve disciples spent alongside Christ, but that this image would no longer apply to them once sent. Effectively, we can easily imagine the apostles proceeding under their own steam, putting into practice without Christ all they had learned from him; but this is quite untrue. In the final two verses of his Gospel, Mark tells us that the Risen Christ ascended into heaven to the right hand of the Father and that the apostles set out on their mission across the earth. Curiously though, to this passage that tells of this separation and dispersal, there is added an essential paradoxical statement, still so true for us today: "The Lord working with them" (16:20).[8]

The synergy of the yoke continues and will continue as long as there are disciples engaged in mission on the earth, even while the Son is seated at the right hand of the Father! Christ is both in heaven and on earth, close to the Father and close to us. The image of the yoke remains and speaks of the unceasing collaboration of the master with his disciples; at the moment he returns to his Father, the Risen Christ says, "I am with you even unto the end of the world" (Matt 28:20).

There is a small theological point to be made here. The Reformers categorically denied any idea of synergy in the work of salvation, in our justification. On the cross, Christ alone is at work. From this fact it is evident that we in no way participate in the work of salvation. This cannot be questioned. However, following the Reformers, where Christ is alone in working our salvation, there is no sanctification without our participation. From the moment the issue is living out the salvation received from Christ, synergy is indispensable.

---

8. The French reads, translated literally, "The Lord was in synergy with them." (Trans.)

And I will give you rest _____

Rest; this is the prospect Jesus envisages for us, in the form of a promise.

In the spiritual life, rest has nothing to do with idleness. This does follow of itself, but it is perhaps good to make the point. Idleness is the daughter of laxity and negligence; it rejects work, flees from it, pushes it away and results in a state of stupor. Rest follows work and is its crown. The more we have worked, the better the rest. Rest, then, reveals the beauty of the work accomplished, and also gives us a glimpse of the joys of the kingdom.

The perspective through which Jesus envisages the period of apprenticeship beneath the yoke is therefore, indeed, rest. What is to be said about this? Is it a matter just of eternal rest at the end of time when the yoke of life has been removed? It is this, but not this alone.

Without looking so far ahead, but also without rejecting this last point, it is possible as a starting point to envisage the rest received from Christ as a present reality, if only in the fact that working as a pair is more restful than working alone, and still more so to work with a companion who is particularly gentle. You will have observed, reader friend, that there are those with whom it is tiring to work, and others with whom the work is restful! To work with Christ, gentle and lowly of heart, is eminently restful. The presence of Christ beside us procures for us rest, even while the yoke is still on our shoulders. To work together with Christ has a restful element to it; this is a gift of Christ, tied to the simple fact of his presence.

Without calling this in question, we need not however limit ourselves to it! The promise of Christ has another bearing altogether. This again concerns the day on which the yoke will be removed, the day when work will be over. Taking off the yoke means entering a time of rest. What a wonderful moment, when the yoke is untied!

The Sabbath rest

In a biblical context, the idea of rest as it relates to work immediately brings us to consider the Sabbath, the day of rest. On this day, the whole world rests, including the servant and the slave, but also the ox and the ass, the beasts of burden *par excellence*; in short, every yoke was lifted. "In six days you shall do your work, but on the seventh you shall rest, that your ox and your ass also may rest" (Exod 23:12). In this verse from Exodus, the allusion to the yoke is still more explicit in the Greek translation of the Septuagint, which translates the word "ass" as *hupozugion*, which is to say, the animal that is "under the yoke." The Septuagint thus reminds us that even the ass must be freed from its yoke to enjoy the Sabbath rest.

The institution of the Sabbath comes from God. It is he who gave this day to humans and to beasts, that they should share the rest he enjoys on this day. ("On the seventh day, God rested from all his work," Gen 2:3). The Sabbath rest is a gift from God, to be enjoyed, savored, and celebrated with him.

Alongside the weekly rest that returns in its regular cycle, God also provides periods of rest to mark the end of times of trial; this was the case, for example, at the end of the Babylonian exile. Days like these are not cyclical but unique, inscribed into human history as further gifts from God, and are also to be savored as times of praise. "When the Lord shall have given you rest, after your pain, your torment, and the hard servitude to which you have been subjected, then you shall take up this proverb against the king of Babylon: The Lord has broken the staff of the wicked!" (Isa 14:3–5). May God be blessed for, in his grace, making provision for our rest.

"I will give you rest," says Jesus. Is this speaking of a rest that is regular and cyclical, or rest that is occasional, or is it perhaps both? I don't really know, but it is certainly the case that Christ enables us to taste, here on earth, moments of rest given by pure grace; indeed he always accomplishes his promise in the reality of our lives, in our human history, so that this rest fills our hearts with thanksgiving.

The final rest

The Sabbath rest is a rest that brings to a close the week of work, but in a temporary way, since the day following the Sabbath, a new week of work begins. The Sabbath rest is intense, lived with God; it is blessed and sanctified by God (Gen 2:3), but it is limited in time. However it announces and prefigures the final rest, also given by God, which will be eternal, the eschatological rest at the end of time. God alone, certainly, can give this rest, this paradisiacal rest.

Of which rest is Jesus thinking in what he says about the yoke? What kind of rest is he promising to give his disciples? A temporary, partial one such as we see for example when he addresses his disciples on their return from their mission: "Come aside into a desert place and rest *for a while*" (Mark 6:31)? Or an eternal, paradisiacal rest?

Why not both? He is altogether capable, indeed, of procuring for us one as well as the other.

The final rest is something we cannot truly imagine, but temporary rest is something we can enjoy. In his grace, indeed, the Lord often lets us taste it in our life as disciples, wonderful moments when the yoke is removed on Christ's initiative, as he himself rests at our side, as in a place apart, a desert place. To rest with him, if only for a while, causes us to thirst for what the final, eternal rest might be.

Rest for the soul

If we are to understand the rest Jesus is speaking of, we need to go a little deeper into the idea, bearing in mind that he states a further specific on which we should pause. "You will find," he says, "rest *unto your souls.*"

Rest . . . for the soul! What does this really mean?

Rest for the body is a reality easily accessible to us. It is not very complicated, indeed, to bring the body to rest. Often just a sofa is enough . . . .

Rest for the spirit is a little more difficult to obtain. I am aware that some people are well able to rest so far as the body is concerned, without ever managing to give rest to their spirit. One might be physically at rest in an armchair while the spirit is still fully active, unable to stop working. We often need time to learn how to rest the spirit, but we do get there all the same.

Rest, repose for the soul is doubtless something else again, but what exactly? And if we ourselves are able to give rest to our body and our spirit, are we able to obtain it for our souls?

The Bible does not say much about rest for the soul! Almost nothing in fact! We have no more on this subject, from the beginning to the end of the Bible, other than the last part of a verse in which the psalmist addresses the following invitation to his soul: "return, o my soul, to your rest" (Ps 116:7). Did his soul respond to this invitation? Did it manage it by its own means? The psalmist doesn't say! We do learn though, that rest for the soul is a reality, even if this reality is fragile and can be lost.

Let us take a look at this unique text, brief though it is, but very instructive. What exactly does the psalmist say to his soul? "Return unto your rest!" This is a mystery. Where is the place of rest for the soul to which it is to return? Assuredly it must be a place that is as invisible and intangible as the soul itself!

The verb "return" used by the psalmist (*shuv*) is very interesting. In the spiritual domain, the word is above all that used for conversion, clearly showing that the return of the soul to its rest is a returning to God, and the place of repose for the soul is doubtless none other than God himself. How true this is! The whole psalm, moreover, becomes clear in this light; rest for the soul is in God and in him alone, because in him and in him only, it knows no conflict, no temptation, no trials, no afflictions, no tribulations, nothing that can compromise or trouble its rest.

Rest like this, God's rest, is properly paradisiacal, such as we know we will experience in fullness at the end of time. This is the final rest, an indescribable rest, beyond words; this is the way Macarius,[9] for example, who was particularly concerned with what this rest for the soul might be, liked to put things.

Something else the psalmist makes plain is that this rest can be enjoyed by the soul on earth, to the degree that here below it can return to God, essentially in repentance. This is right, with the condition that we not believe that the acquisition of rest relies on the good will of the soul alone, on its decision alone, its initiative alone, its own effort alone, its own exertions, its own good works of repentance, but, in the end on . . . the rest of Christ

The rest of Christ

In a beautiful homily[10] Macarius points away from this error with a very just development of the theme, centering the problem on the one essential, the cross. If it is possible for the soul to return to God in repentance and know rest, this is all thanks to Christ, Christ who on the cross redeemed our souls. Macarius continues that, having bought our souls, Christ has made them his dwelling place and the place of his rest! This is a great squaring of accounts, but also a wonderful and un-expected turnaround; the soul, says Macarius, knows rest when Christ comes to rest within it because the soul is the place of Christ's rest.

9. Fourth-century Egyptian monk, to whom the works now known as Pseudo-Macarius were originally ascribed. (Trans.)

10. No. 16 in collection III, in Pseudo-Macarius, *Oeuvres spirituelles* [Spiritual Works] (Sources chrètiennes 275. Paris: Cerf, 1980), 179.

This is a great marvel; that Christ be the soul's resting place, and the soul the resting place of Christ! The soul finds its rest in the rest Christ gives as he rests in it!

"I will give you rest." What Macarius says fits well with this perspective. It is indeed Christ who gives the soul rest, not the soul obtaining rest for itself through its conversion.

Rest for our soul; before he gives it to us, Christ desires it more than do we, since he has suffered much more than we to obtain it. He suffered the cross; he has paid the price of his life to make our hearts his place of rest. Where Christ looks to find rest in us, it is as a resting-place following the battle of the cross:

> He greatly desires to take rest within his own house, in our bodies and in our souls; he, the beautiful and only Spouse, the Christ, who underwent so much pain for us and has bought us with his own blood. He is always knocking at the door of our hearts, that we may open to him, that he may enter and find rest in our souls and establish there his dwelling place.[11]

Christ knocks at our door that we may open freely to him and respond to his desire with our desire, to his love with our love. The process is initiated by Christ and not by us, whose place it is nevertheless to respond freely. Then the Spouse enters his dwelling place, and Macarius no longer knows whether to speak of the rest of the soul or the rest of Christ since the two are inseparable. "Having the hope of the coming and rest of the Lord in our souls, or rather, the rest of our souls in the Lord . . . ."[12] The rest of our soul here on earth is both the rest of Christ in us and our rest in him, which is truly paradisiacal, indescribable, beyond words . . . .

Anyone who has tasted the rest of the soul with Christ has no desire other than to taste it afresh. But why would it be lost? Because grace draws back the moment it is disturbed. What is it that comes to trouble our rest? There are quite simply a host of intruders; all the

11. Ibid., 193.
12. Ibid., 201.

seductions that we allow in our wandering, our simplicity, our foolish sinfulness . . . . The soul, in fact, in its weakness will open the door a little to almost anything; there are so many evil spirits, in any case, that seek to seduce it, to render it a slave to the passions! Unfortunates that we are!

What is so great in this homily of Macarius is that the two rests—that of the soul and that of Christ—are inseparable, as inseparable as is everything experienced beneath the same yoke. Something still more beautiful though is to see the degree to which Macarius is concerned more with Christ's rest than with his own. This is real love, despoiled of all spiritual egotism; just as Jesus is concerned with the rest of those he invites to take up his yoke, so too, Macarius, as a disciple, is concerned with the rest of his Lord.

Happy the disciple who has greater thirst for their master's rest than for their own!

How are we to enable Christ to find rest in us? By ridding our souls of all that repels his presence, everything that ties us to the passions. This work, most happily for us, is something he accomplishes with us, by his grace, certainly, but this is his *work*, not his rest!

Obstacles to the soul's rest

Impossible though it is to describe the soul's rest, it is quite possible to describe the state of a soul that does not know rest.

According to the Bible, the soul is the seat of the desires. In so far as some desire is not satisfied, the soul is not at rest. Now, the desires of the soul are multiple; some of these may be being met, but it only needs one to be unmet for the soul to fail to find rest. The ultimate desire of the soul, the deepest, the one that, once satisfied, enables the soul to have fullness of rest, is the desire for God. One thing is therefore clear, that God is the only one who can satisfy the deep desire of the soul, and so the only one who can truly give the soul rest; the deep rest in God causes all other desires to disappear.

Happy are those able, with the psalmist, to tell God of this desire which is so deep: "My soul longs after you, O God!" (Ps 42:2). They are happy because they will hear Christ reply, "Come unto me, all of you, and I will give you rest. Come, and you will find rest for your souls."

The soul is no longer at rest when it stands in need of forgiveness. Remorse, guilt, prevent it knowing rest. True forgiveness is the forgiveness that God alone can give; we understand this with the discovery that, in the Hebrew, the verb for forgive (*sālakh*) only ever has God as its subject. God alone, indeed, is able to truly and perfectly bring pardon to the depths of the soul; the psalmist understood this as he speaks to his soul: "Bless the Lord, o my soul, for it is he who forgives all your sins" (103:2–3). When Jesus promises the soul to procure its rest, this is because he, as God himself, is the bearer of God's pardon (Mark 2:7).

Fear too can trouble the soul and estrange it from rest. The soul can be assailed by a multiplicity of fears; the fear of God's condemnation or abandonment by him, or, again, the fear of death, or still others . . . . Nothing can cause these fears to dissipate except perfect love, as John says (1 John 4:16), that is, the love of God. Yes, God alone is capable of bringing peace to the soul's trouble by delivering it from its fears.[13] Only God is thus able to give the soul rest.

"Come unto me, all you who are weary and heavy laden, weighed down with remorse or guilt, exhausted by the assaults of worry and fear, all you who are thirsty for God! Come unto me and you will find rest for your souls!" If Jesus speaks like this, it is because he is God.

Tiredness from spiritual travail

We have not yet said everything about the thirst for rest a soul may feel. "Come unto me, all you who are weary and heavy laden." Jesus

13. Ps 34:4–5. (Trans.)

speaks to "all" the weary and "all" the heavy laden, to all those who in their soul also experience the weariness of spiritual travail and battle, since, doubtless, it is this that most fatigues the soul, the incessant battle against evil thoughts, against impure thoughts, thoughts sown in us by powers that wish to separate us from God and estrange God from our soul, the place of his rest. This incessant travail, Jesus comes to accomplish with us as he binds himself to the same yoke as us, as he whispers to our heart that he promises us always to be at rest. To the degree the soul is assailed by passionate thoughts, led around by the passions, it has no rest.

Without Christ, this labor leads to discouragement and despair since the soul does not have sufficient resources in itself to carry on the struggle satisfactorily. With Christ as yoke companion, in synergy with the strength of Christ, in synergy with the strength of his love, the soul can shoulder the fatigue of spiritual combat and stay strong until the moment it is enabled to enjoy rest. The one who gives the soul rest is the same as he who, beneath the yoke, joins his strength to ours. Only he, in his grace, decides at what moment to undo the yoke for a time of rest.

Happy the soul that here on earth receives rest from Christ and enjoys it with him since it already sees the joy of the kingdom. Happy, even when it is only a moment of rest, a brief time out, because it then takes up the yoke again with multiplied strength.

Rest in God

While Macarius recognizes that the rest of the soul is indescribable, he nevertheless endeavors to describe it a little, using a very suggestive image drawn from John's Gospel. The soul has rest, he says, when it lies in the bosom of Christ: "Lord, hide me at your right hand and cause me to rest on your bosom."[14]

14. Pseudo-Macarius, *Oeuvres spirituelles*, 91.

This image is superb because it clearly shows that this rest can be a reality during our time here on earth, even if only for short periods, just as the well-beloved disciple truly knew—right here—rest on the bosom of his Lord (John 13:23). A wonderful image, because it also implies the idea that Christ himself must be at rest since the soul finds rest on his breast. We have seen this, that rest is shared; the one who gives it and the one who receives it savor the rest together, which is still more beautiful and profound given that the weariness and pain were also shared beneath the same yoke.

When, though, is Christ himself at rest? It is very simple; when he himself is on the bosom of the Father (John 1:18). It is there, on the bosom of Father, that the Son finds the depths of his rest. The rest the Son gives is the rest he receives from his Father and shares with him. If the Son, indeed, knows rest on the bosom of his Father, it is because the Father himself is at rest in receiving his Son in this way. It is this rest, shared with his Father, that the Son gives to whoever rests on his bosom. What depths there are to such rest . . . !

"If anyone loves me," says Jesus, "he will keep my word, and my Father will love him; we will come to him, we will make our home with him" (John 14:23). "At home with him . . . !" This is to say, in his soul, as Macarius so justly comments. Not only is the soul the place of rest of the Son, but also of the Father . . . . What an unspeakable wonder!

The Father, the Son, at rest . . . but what of the Holy Spirit? Does he also know rest? Yes, Macarius tells us, and then specifies, "The Spirit's place of rest is where there is humility, love, gentleness, and all else commanded by the Lord."[15] This is wonderful; gentleness, humility . . . the very qualities Christ specifies and which he wishes to reveal to us beneath the yoke! The Spirit, then, finds his repose in Christ, just as he does in the soul to whom Christ has taught gentleness and humility.

---

15. *Les homélies spirituelles de saint Macarie: Le Saint-Esprit et le chrétien* [Spiritual Homilies of Saint Macarius: The Holy Spirit and the Christian]. French translation with an Introduction by Father Placide Deseille (Edition abbaye de Bellefontaine Spiritualité Orientale 40. Maine-et-Loire: Abbaye de Bellefontaine, 1984), 226.

Rest for the soul . . . it lies in Christ, in whom repose the Father and the Spirit . . . . Macarius was right to say that it is beyond description; an inexpressible, ineffable rest which immerses the soul in the unfathomable mystery of the Trinity . . . .

One last word, before we enjoy the silence of worship . . . .

The Father revealed

The image of the yoke immediately follows Jesus saying this: "No one knows the Son except the Father, and no one knows the Father except the Son and those to whom he will reveal him."

"And those to whom he will reveal him," which is to say, those to whom the Son will reveal the Father. This last expression spoken by Jesus precedes the invitation he addresses to all those who are weary and heavy laden to become his disciples.

To whom then will the Son reveal the Father? Surely, it will be those who come to him, who will take upon themselves his yoke and who will thus become his disciples, learning from him how gentle and lowly of heart he is.

What is it of the Father that will be revealed? Above all, that the gentleness and humility set forward in Christ, the gentleness and lowliness of the Son are the gentleness and humility of the Father, because the Son is the perfect image of the Father . . . .

The Father, gentle and lowly of heart! This is a real revelation, a wonderful revelation!

One has to have worked under the yoke, alongside the Son, to receive this revelation . . . .

It is an indescribable revelation which is received in the inexpressible rest of the soul, on the bosom of the Son, on the bosom of the Father . . . .

The Father . . . gentle and lowly of heart . . . .

— CHAPTER 3 —

Abide in Me

W HEN HE CALLED HIS disciples, Jesus invited them to follow him, to march *behind* him. Later he invited them to come a little nearer, to come *alongside* him, to take up the same yoke. Finally, on the evening before his passion, believing that his disciples were ready to hear something still greater, Jesus began to speak to them of a bond of unsurpassable depth, not simply "behind" him, not "alongside" him, but *"in"* him!

> *I am the true vine and my Father is the vinedresser. Every branch in me that does not bear fruit he takes away, and every branch that bears fruit he prunes that it may bear more fruit. You have already been pruned by the word that I have spoken to you. Abide in me, as I abide in you. As the branch cannot bear fruit of itself if it does not abide in the vine, no more can you if you do not abide in me. I am the vine and you are the branches. Whoever abides in me and I in them bears plenty of fruit, because without me you can do nothing. If anyone does not abide in me, they are cast out as a branch and wither; then the branches are gathered together and thrown into the fire and burnt. If you abide in me and my words abide in you, ask whatever you wish and it will be granted you. In this my Father will be glorified, that you bear plenty of fruit, and that you become my disciples.*
>
> *As the Father has loved me, so have I loved you; abide in my love. If you keep my commandments, you will abide in my love, just as I have kept the commandments of my Father, and I abide in his love. I have told you these things that my joy may be in you and*

that your joy may be complete. This is my commandment, that you love one another as I have loved you. There is no greater love than to lay down your life for your friends. You are my friends if you do what I command you to do. I do not call you servants, because the servant does not know what his master is doing, but I have called you friends, because everything that I have heard from my Father I have made known to you. It is not you who have chosen me but I who have chosen you, and I have established you that you may go and bear fruit, and that your fruit may remain, so that whatever you ask the Father in my name, he will give it you. My command is that you love one another. (John 15:1–17)

"Whoever abides in me, and in him (or her)" (v. 5). In this relationship established between Jesus and the disciple it is no longer a case of following "behind" Christ, or even marching "alongside" him, but of being "in" Christ and Christ being "in" the disciple.

The bond that here becomes apparent with Jesus is that of mutual inhabitation, of a communion that is altogether exceptional, absolutely unique; but it needs clarification, and this is what Jesus provides as he develops the image of the vine and its branches.

We in him and he in us; what is this saying? No rabbi before him had ever said such a thing!

The sap, the life force, is love

The strong bond that unites the vine and the branches has to do with the sap that flows through them. Jesus does not here use the word "sap," but nonetheless gives a lengthy excursus on love in a way suggestive of the sap in a vine; this is because he speaks of the love flowing in just one direction, from Christ towards the disciples, not in the reverse direction, just as the sap flows from the vine into the branches and not the other way round. The whole picture is centered on the love that flows and gives life, like the sap in a plant.

"I have loved you," Jesus says twice (vv. 9 and 12), using the perfect tense, which expresses not so much a concluded reality as its indeterminate duration.[1] Christ's love for his disciples will continue indefinitely. Jesus asks nothing of them in return, underlining the free nature of his love, like the sap, which provides the branches with all they need, without receiving anything in return.

What Jesus does ask of his disciples is not that they love him back, but that they diffuse, spread his love to others, to share what they have received from him: "that you love one another" (vv. 12 and 17).

This love lavished in first place by Christ upon the branches does not truly come from him, since he himself receives it from his Father; but Jesus does not feel the need to speak here of the love for the Father he gives in return, thereby keeping close to the picture of the sap flowing in just the one direction: "the Father has loved me" (v. 9).

Love appears here, then, like an immense one-directional current, originating in the Father, passing through the Son, and spreading among the disciples. To be sure, the reciprocal nature of love is not being denied by Jesus, who speaks of it in other texts, but he is underlining here, thanks to the image he chooses, this flowing stream from God to humans through his intermediary.

Allowing yourself to be loved

This way of speaking about love invites the disciple to understand that we receive before we give; that we are not the origin of the love, and that we are loved before we love. It is an invitation to learn something the disciple often has trouble putting into practice: to allow ourselves first to be loved by Christ, before attempting to ourselves love.

---

1. The best translation would be "I love you"; nevertheless, in French (as in English—Trans.) this is a little too abrupt, lacking the delicacy preserved by the present perfect; but the meaning is indeed simply present.

Allowing oneself to be loved by Christ, to be loved by God through Christ, is opening oneself to this love, just as the branch opens to the sap it receives from the vine and which gives it life. How easy this is for the branch, and how difficult for us! We have so much trouble accepting being loved by Christ, welcoming this love that Christ lavishes upon us and which gives us life!

How blessed we are if we thirst for the love of Christ as the branch thirsts for the sap.

Allowing ourselves to be loved by Christ means opening up to him, committing ourselves to him, abandoning ourselves to him in full confidence, knowing that his love is for every day and not occasional, that it is continuing like the sap in the branch, but also hidden, unseen, and even imperceptible, beyond our awareness . . . . Nevertheless, even if it is more often than not unperceived, Jesus tells us there is no greater love than his.

"There is no greater love than to lay down your life for your friends" (v. 13). When the disciples heard this, the cross was still future; they had as yet no true measure of the depths of this gift, no way as yet of knowing how the statement "I have loved you" would be amplified, how the future would overshadow the past and the present. They had no idea of it, nor could they begin to estimate it because this love is really beyond measure! To suggest the depth of his love, Jesus contents himself with taking as his reference another love, the extent of which also defies definition: "as the Father has loved me . . . ."

How can it be that we should find it so difficult to allow ourselves to be loved by a love that is so great, love that has its origin in God, a love that is divine? It's because the love goes infinitely beyond us, surely, but also because we have so many reticences, brakes, blockages, and at times even refusals . . . . How long it takes to become truly a disciple, fully a disciple, much longer than for a branch to be a branch!

Happy is the person who knows him or herself loved unceasingly, day and night, infinitely! Happy is the one who knows that the love of Christ is fully sufficient for life, and who lives by this!

The fruit

While the word "sap" is not employed in the picture, the issue of fruit is abundantly present (vv. 2, 4, 5, 8, 16). The word "fruit" is always found here in the singular, but it is a collective singular, so it has a plural sense.

Speaking with such insistence about fruit places an emphasis on the branches rather than the vine. You will never indeed see grapes growing directly from the vine trunk; the grapes are all on the branches. The only thing looked for from the vine is the fruit, and it is only found on the branches. How humble Christ is, retiring entirely into the background and honoring his disciples to the highest degree!

Nevertheless, Jesus recalls to their senses anyone with a tendency to bypass him: "without me you can do nothing" (v. 5). Tell me, though, what branch would ever dream of doing without the vine to produce grapes? No way! However, what no branch would dream of thinking, we, all the same, manage to consider!

"Without me," which is to say, if you do not abide in me and I in you, you can't do anything. Fruit is the product of our love communion with Christ, the result of an indispensable synergy that is both mysterious and necessary; without the vine the branch cannot produce fruit; without the branch, the vine cannot do so either; this profound communion between the two is necessary if there is to be fruit.

The image is that everything that a disciple might do without Christ is of no account, and not even of interest. We can begin to think that, in our lives, there is a life alongside our Christian life, a part of our life that is independent of our bond with Christ! This idea, though, is totally excluded, not just here in the image of the vine, but throughout Jesus' teaching. Nowhere is there any such idea; for Jesus, life outside of him has no interest; it does not even exist!

Bearing fruit

"Without me you can do nothing": the accent is placed here on the word "do," on what the disciples can do with Christ. This emphasis would be expected to point the image of the vine towards the expression "make[2] fruit," which is an expression current in the Greek in the sense of "produce fruit." This expression is by far the one most commonly found in the Gospels, as we see for example in Matthew 3:8, 10; 7:17, etc. . . . But curiously, although Jesus says, "without me you can do nothing," he never here uses the expression "to make fruit." He systematically pushes that idea aside, replacing it each time with another, less common, expression, "to bear fruit" (vv. 2, 4, 5, 8, 16).[3] We might see this as a somewhat humorous way to inoculate the disciples against any eventual attack of pride! It is not the disciple who "makes" the fruit he produces. No, he does nothing but "bear" it! It is understood that the one who in truth makes, produces, the fruit is the vine, that is, Christ. It is only implied, because of the extreme humility of Christ who does not push to the fore what he does!

Happy is the disciple who is humble enough to remember that he (or she),[4] in reality, produces nothing; that all he does is bear what Christ brings to realization through him! A disciple like this truly knows how to live in love communion with his Lord. How impoverished, though, is the disciple who wishes to take as his own fruit that is not his, but which instead he receives from the one who abides in him, and in whom he ought to abide!

---

2. This cannot really be translated into English; the point is that French has one word, *faire*, which means both "do" and "make." (Trans.)

3. The author points out in his note that he is disappointed the French TOB translation was not more careful at this point; ". . . each time, it translates here with the phrase 'produce fruit,' which can only bring confusion to the reader's mind." Most English translations seem to use "bear," but a few of them say "produce." "Bear" is clearly more passive than "produce" and therefore better. (Trans.)

4. In all that follows, please understand 'he' to include 'she'; at times it is difficult to be suitably inclusive in English without being impersonal and clumsy. (Trans.)

A miracle of humility _____

The fruit is a miracle which results from love communion with Christ. This miracle is of the same sort as that which took place the day the bread was multiplied. On that day, who was it that multiplied the bread? Well, Jesus, certainly; but he set about it in such a way that the miracle took place in the hands of the disciples. Jesus was happy to take the bread, to give thanks to his Father, from whom he received everything, and then break the bread and give it to the disciples for them to distribute. That's all! It was in the hands of the disciples that the miracle was manifest in everyone's sight. Jesus stepped back behind his disciples in such a way that he seems to have needed them to bring the miracle to pass. Let us not, however, be fooled; without Christ, the disciples would never have been able to perform this distributive miracle! It was the case that "without me you can do nothing."

So where does the fruit come from? From the vine that produces it or the branch that bears it? The humble branch would say it is the fruit of the vine, and the humble vine would say it is the fruit of the branch. I don't know what you would say, reader friend, about the fruit that you bear in your life, but I know one thing, that Christ is sufficiently humble never to speak in this text of "*my* fruit." He concludes this passage wonderfully, saying, "I have chosen you and established you, that you should go and bear fruit and that *your* fruit remain" (v. 16).

How wonderful you are, Lord, in your humility! In your communion of love with us, you are so humbly united with us that you attribute to us all that you work through us . . . .

It is a wonder to contemplate here the humility of Christ, and also to contemplate it in the events of our lives; a wonder to discover that all we do in his name comes from him, that our actions and words of love contain the love of Christ for those towards whom we turn. All that flows out of our love for others is, above all, the love of Christ for them.

Christ is so humble that he hides himself in order to love through us! He hides himself to such a degree that he does so without our knowing it! So often it is only after the act that we discover the truth with wonderment!

Happy is he or she who finds in himself the fruit of Christ's love for others. Happy is he who, when he discovers this, attributes nothing to himself. Happy is she who, without this discovery, continues to love others, applying herself always to abiding in Christ.

The work of the vinedresser

The image of the vine is archetypal in the Old Testament as a description of God's love for his people. "I will sing the song of my well-beloved for his vineyard"; in this way, the prophet Isaiah describes the incomparable love of God for Israel (Isa 5:1). Clearing the land, ridding it of stones, planting, building a tower, digging out a press . . . everything God does in his vineyard is solely dictated by love.

"My Father is the vinedresser," says Jesus, and sets himself very centrally within the biblical tradition. From this, given that we are talking about God's vineyard, it is clear that whatever the vinedresser does will be dictated by love. It's important not to forget this as we read Jesus' description of his Father's labors in his vineyard.

As we read the text, we realize that the whole of the vinedresser's labor is focused on the fruit, that the harvest be the best possible, even though this might not be so evident to the branches. In fact, the vinedresser prunes some and cuts out others, according to whether or not they bear fruit. Whether cut out or pruned, the objective is always that the maximum of sap reach the fruit; we want the fruit to grow. Cutting out or pruning, something is always taken away, but to augment the result; always something less, with something more in view!

However, from the point of view of the branches, whether you are cut off or pruned, it still simply represents a snip with the secateurs!

Either way, the verbs suggest pain for the branches, the pain of removal of what would shade the fruit. It is a suffering, certainly, but dictated by love. Love for the vine will inevitably work this way. Everything that is not the fruit of love is to be cast aside! Everything superfluous, ostentatious, void of love, this is what the Father applies himself to doing away with! Pride and vainglory are particularly in view here, as is everything that is a stranger to love.

When we understand that it is out of love, and that love may grow, that God takes hold of everything in our lives contrary to love, then we accept the wounds of the secateurs, the deprivations and renunciations that this implies, even though accompanied by a certain degree of pain. The branch's place is simply to abandon itself to the work of the vinedresser in total confidence because it proceeds out of love, from the quality of love. Genuine love is able to bear any pain that accompanies its growth and purification. Further to this, "to purify" is the other sense of the Greek verb translated as "prune."[5] To prune a branch is to purify a disciple. Human love has an unceasing need to be purified, even though this is sure to be attended by some pain.

Happy is he or she who lets himself be pruned, purified so that the work of Christ in him may grow! Happy is he or she who welcomes the purifying work of God and gives thanks!

As an offering to the vinedresser

Who is the fruit for when harvest time comes? It is not for the vine, nor indeed for the branch, but for the vinedresser! Neither the vine nor the branch has ever been seen to eat a grape! The fruit the vine produces and the branch bears is for the vinedresser, for his joy, for his

5. This is why the translations are uncertain how to render this verb. In verse 3, the TOB translates, "you have already been pruned," but Segond, "you are already clean." Both translations are correct, but neither of them really gets across the fullness of the Greek. In the absence of a better translation in French [as in English], the important thing is to note and bear in mind the richness of the Greek.

pleasure. The best of the vine and the branch is to be an offering to the vinedresser.

Happy is the disciple who offers all his or her fruit to the Father, marveling at having been able to bear it, and thanking Christ for having produced it in him.

This is not stated in the Gospel text, but a vineyard worker made me aware that right where the branch is pruned, the sap begins to flow. It is then said that the branch "weeps." The branch's tear, in a way, reveals its suffering, but, in another way, the tear reveals its vitality. The branch is indeed alive! Quickly enough the branch ceases to weep and redirects all its sap towards the fruit. The tear shed by the branch will not have been a tear lost in vain; in fact, it will have reassured the vinedresser of his vine's good health . . . .

How does God prune us?

Only the vinedresser does the pruning! Anything else that might damage the branch (the wind, an animal, a passer-by . . .) does not constitute pruning. In short, not everything in our lives of a painful nature is God's purifying. We need to think here only about what God does.

I am not going to tell you how the work of pruning is done in a vineyard! In our lives as disciples, though, how does God undertake to prune, to cleanse us? What, in the end, corresponds to the cut of the secateurs?

The answer to this question is given by Jesus himself: "You are already clean through the word that I have spoken to you" (v. 3). This is what cleanses us, the word of Christ, his gospel, his good news of love. It is true that some of Jesus' words are often difficult to understand, to receive, to put into practice, and that this is not always achieved without suffering; but it is also true that a loving word can heal our flawed ability to love, nurse it, purify it, disinfect it.

There are some pains we accept from a doctor because we know they are salutary. The Lord, the doctor of our souls, cares for us and heals us by his word. He heals anything in our love that is sick, soiled, gangrenous, in a wonderful cleansing that restores us to good health.

Through the word of Christ working within us, it is the Father who is at work. The word does not operate on its own, but the Father works through it.

"That my words abide in you" is Jesus' desire (v. 7). If he longs for this, it is so that the Father may pursue his work in us.

Happy is he or she in whom the Word dwells without ceasing, and who allows himself through its medium to be stripped and cleansed by God.

A word about prayer

"If my words abide in you, ask whatever you wish and it will be granted you" (v. 7). Very clearly, the issue here is prayer, even though the word doesn't appear in this phrase. We need to read very carefully, because what Jesus is saying here on the subject is of great importance, but it can lead to confusion.

One of the great misunderstandings about prayer and its fulfillment comes from the tendency to pray without taking sufficient account of Jesus and his teaching. "If my words abide in you, ask . . . ." Jesus clearly specifies here that prayer is an extension of his own word. Answered prayer is therefore that of the disciple who is indwelt by Jesus' words, the disciple who is full of them and lives by them, to the point where his or her prayer flows from them as their logical extension, not as an expression of whims, dreams, or desires, however praiseworthy.

"If you abide in me and my words abide in you . . . ," Jesus further specifies. Our Lord reaffirms here the deep and indispensable communion between him and his disciple. Prayer is therefore seen as fruit, one of the fruits of this profound communion of love, and so, a fruit we bear and that Christ produces; so much so that prayer can be considered as issuing from him in us and that, in a way, it is he who prays in us. That said, when Christ prays like this in us, then there is a fulfillment of this prayer, which is at once both his and ours. How can we be sure that our prayer is indeed his? By abiding in him, by living from his words and in his words.

"Abide in me"; this is the number one thing that Christ has to say about what we are to do before we begin to pray.

Prayer that issues from Christ's words is therefore a fruit of the vine and of the branches, a fruit of the vineyard, just like every work of love. For the vinedresser, it is fruit for him to harvest, a delightful fruit that it is his pleasure to honor. God fulfills prayer because there is nothing of greater price in his eyes than what is born of the communion between Christ and his disciples.

If you keep my commandments

Jesus continues with the theme of his word, and now strengthens what he is saying. Here it is not a matter of what he says as a whole but of his commandments alone; by inviting us to keep his commandments Jesus raises the issue of our obedience.

"If you keep my commandments, you will abide in my love" (v. 10). A poor interpretation of this verse, isolating it from its context, would give us to understand that the love of Christ for us depends on our obedience, that it is a recompense, a payment, as if it were necessary to obey to obtain Christ's love. This is a deplorable misunderstanding, turning love into bargaining!

When we consider the whole passage closely, Jesus begins by affirming his love for his disciples as a working reality; it is a particular love, one which does not bargain, a love as great as his Father's love for him; "as the Father has loved me, I have loved you" (v. 9). Only after establishing this love as a foundation does Jesus invite his disciples to "abide" in this love (v. 10), not to enter it, but to stay there, to continue to be loved by him. How? By living his word, by putting it into practice. That is what obedience is, putting into practice Christ's word of love, the expression of the love communion with him, the outworking of that communion, the result of taking it seriously, its manifestation, its concrete form. To obey is to perpetuate the love, to turn the present into the eternal. When we obey Christ, it is not *so that* he love us, but because he *already* loves us, with a love equal to that he enjoys with the Father.

Such a vision of obedience is altogether free of any suggestion of bargaining; it is also free of all legalism, because it is full of love. Legalism is obedience devoid of love, an obedience that becomes its own goal.

The obedience of friends

The obedience Jesus envisages is not just any obedience, as he is about to say. As he speaks of his love for his disciples, Jesus does not describe them as servants; a servant is not necessarily loved by his master. Jesus states clearly that he is addressing his disciples as friends; "you are my friends" (v. 14).

> This is not a friendship that will crown your life of obedience, but one that will crown the gift of my life. It is because I am giving my life for you that you will understand the degree to which I love you, the degree to which you are my friends. In friendship there is reciprocity, without which the friendship is not shared. As you understand in my death for you how much of a friend I am to you, so I will understand through your obedience this same friendship. If you wish to demonstrate your friendship with me concretely, this is what you can do—do what I ask you.

The obedience of a friend has nothing to do with that of a servant. It is disinterested; it does not seek to buy off its master to avoid his anger or rebukes; it thirsts to give love; it exerts itself to demonstrate love, to the point of seeking to forestall any request. A true friend does not wait for a request to be made of him, but attempts to pre-empt, to forestall, to give what has not yet been asked, to do what has not been commanded . . . out of love! Obedience like this has for a model the obedience of Christ to his Father. It's no doubt because we are unaware of what Christ's friendship is that we have so much trouble understanding obedience.

Christ's friendship

We can become servants overnight by means of a simple work contract. We do not become friends overnight! It requires time, lengthy shared experience, lengthy companionship . . . .

Jesus awaited his final day before speaking to his disciples of his friendship because it needed time to be born and woven. It needed three years, time spent on the Galilee roads, in the desert places and storms, through the course of festivals and the daily routine. Now the time had come to talk about it.

No disciple would ever, of himself, have dreamt of becoming Christ's friend. To recognize him as the Son of God suggests the removal of the shoes, prostration before him, honoring him as God, not telling him that he's our friend! It's on the lips of Jesus that the word "friend" appears. It is he who chooses this love relationship, not the disciples; "it is I who have chosen you, not you me" (v. 16).

Friendship is not something to be claimed or bought, negotiated or litigated . . . it is welcomed with wonderment, in the silence of wonderment; life is altogether transformed by it. It is welcomed in silence in a transformed obedience.

This is exactly how the disciples received the friendship of Christ, in silence! Where they had asked questions at the outset of Jesus' farewell discourse, as any good disciple would ask of his master, now, after what they have just heard, they ask nothing more; they ponder in silence the one they are discovering to be their friend . . . !

The friend of the bridegroom

One person alone, prior to this final evening, had spoken of friendship with Christ, but it's possible that no one paid any attention to his comments since it was at the outset of Jesus' ministry. We should now listen again to the man who spoke this way.

"The friend of the bridegroom stands by and listens to him, and the voice of the bridegroom fills him with joy; this is my joy and my joy is full" (John 3:29). It was John the Baptist who said this, and who considered himself a friend of Christ.

What fills the Baptist with joy is the voice of Christ, not simply the content of the words, but just the sound of his voice. This is so true; to recognize the voice of a friend produces great joy. When the friend in question is Christ, the joy is so great that it is "full, perfect," as John testifies.

After the Baptist, the disciples are also to become friends of Christ and know the same joy, just as Jesus told them: "I have told you these things that my joy might be in you, and that your *joy* might be *full*" (v. 11).

Anyone who knows the perfect joy of friendship advances his joy towards fulfillment by looking to pre-empt his friend's slightest desire.

Happy, a thousand times happy, is he, or she, who recognizes Jesus simply by the sound of his voice.

John the Baptist also tells us how he put into practice his friendship with Christ, opening a way on the road still so unknown to us; "he must increase and I must decrease" (3:30). The humility of friendship; this truly is perfect joy!

Abide in me

Jesus never said to his disciple, *"be* in me"; it was not the disciples' job to accomplish that; it was the Father's business alone. To be in Christ is to be a new creature; this is the work of God, and why the Son turns to his Father and addresses this prayer to him: "May they be in us" (John 17:21).

The vine never says to the branches, "be in me," because they already are, from the word go! Jesus has never said to the disciples "be in me," because they already are, by the Father's grace. He simply tells them, and for him it is enough that he says it, "abide in me."

It is the Father's place to see that the disciples be in Christ. It is the disciples' concern to abide in him, to remain in what they are by the Father's power, to persevere with the Father's help. We are already in Christ by baptism; it is incumbent upon us in our lives as baptized persons to abide in Christ, with the help of God.

Neither does Jesus ever ask his disciples to abide in each other. The profound communion with Christ does not exist among the disciples without Christ as intermediary. Indeed, at a human level, it is never the case that anyone can be in another and the other in him. The communion Jesus talks about does not exist at a human level. If it is possible with Christ, it is because he is not only a man but also God. This now needs to be defined.

What is the pattern for communion?

"Abide in me and I in you"; what exactly is the nature of the communion Jesus speaks of here? It is certainly illuminated by the image of the vine and the branches, but this is only an image. Is there a model in human relations that would further enable an understanding of what Jesus is saying, a pattern of communion with the same reciprocity, the same mutual life?

The closest communion between two people, the closest love relation, is certainly that between a man and a woman in marriage, between spouses. To express this communion of love, the Old Testament uses a very significant expression found in the Song of Songs, the book of love, also based on reciprocity: "My beloved is mine and I am his" (Song 2:16).

This indeed is reciprocity, a mutual bond. The phrasing is very close to that used by Jesus, but not as deep. A spouse indeed "belongs" to his beloved, and she "belongs" to him. This communion, though, is never great enough for us to say that one is "in" the other and the other "in" him. Conjugal communion in Hebrew is expressed by the particle *le*, denoting "belonging," never by *be*, "in." "To belong to" is never as strong or as deep as "to be *in.*"

The Old Testament speaks of another bond of communion, one just as deep, that which unites God to his people. Here too there is a characteristic turn of phrase denoting a very strong tie. It is found in different prophets, for example Jeremiah, spoken by God as he addresses Israel: "I will be to them their God, and they shall be to me my people" (31:32). Here again, though, it is a "belonging to" the other, not a "being in" the other. Never in the Old Testament is there any question of a communion that would be still stronger, where God would be "in" his people and the people "in" God.

A third mutual bond, also very strong, appears in the Old Testament, that between God and the Messiah, the son of David. This bond is described in another phrase which instances a reciprocity of mutual love, but the expression never goes beyond those we have looked at. This is what God says with regard to the offspring of David: "I will be to him a father, and he will be to me as a son" (2 Sam 7:14). Here the bond is not conjugal but filial, but it is still expressed with the particle *le* not *be*. It is never said that God will be "in" the Messiah, nor the Messiah "in" him.

Jesus is therefore bringing an innovation! He is obliged to do so since there is no model for communion at his disposal across the range of human relations that would make it any clearer what he is asking of his disciples; "abide in me, and I in you." While he had a genius for parables, setting forth different characters in various types of relationship (king and subjects, masters and servants, father and son . . .) he doesn't suggest any such illustration here. The lack of any appropriate human point of reference no doubt explains why he now complements what he says with an image from the plant kingdom.

Jesus innovates, invents, speaks of a bond of fellowship of which no one had ever spoken before and which goes beyond all others in depth. But how were the disciples to understand what they were being invited into?

The Father and the Son

When Jesus speaks to his disciples, it is the final evening of his life, the day before his death. He reveals to them this bond of communion, certainly undreamt of by them, but not totally enigmatic, in so far as he bases what he says on another bond, one he had already spoken to them about well before this final evening: "The Father is in me and I am in the Father" (John 10:38).

"The Father is in me and I am in the Father"; the day Jesus made this declaration it left the disciples speechless, as one can readily understand. The communion he speaks of is in fact so unique and exalted that, beyond question, it exceeds all understanding! However, it is so clearly revealed by Christ that we can't ignore it. No one before Jesus had ever spoken of such a bond with God; it is a bond that is more than human . . . .

This then is the pattern for communion, the only model that can shed light on our bond with Christ. It doesn't exist at a human level but is found in God, in the deepest place in God, in the unfathomable mystery of communion between the Father and the Son. What Jesus says about his bond with the Father goes well beyond what God himself had said about his bond with the Messiah. Jesus does not just "belong" to the Father or the Father to him, but he is "in" the Father and the Father "in" him. This is a deep mystery never approached outside of God!

"The Father is in me, and I am in the Father"; the day Jesus said this he had also just made another statement, "I and the Father are one" (10:30). While the disciples were speechless, some of the Jews gathered stones with which to stone Jesus. We understand this too; what he is saying, in fact, sounds very much like blasphemy! For someone to speak like this he must be mocking God or indeed . . . himself be God!

"The Father is in me, and I am in the Father"; this expression is still more concise in the Greek, where there is no verb: "the Father in me, and I in the Father." It could not be more concise, stronger, or more mysterious! It is only in what follows that Jesus makes the nature of the bond a little more explicit by using the verb "abide" and even the verb "be"; this is of great importance since it concerns the very essence of God: "I in the Father and the Father is in me . . . the Father abides in me" (John 14:10).

The Father in the Son and the Son in the Father; there is nothing in the nature of fusion in this affirmation. The Son indeed will never cease to be the Son or the Father to be the Father. The bond between them has neither confusion nor separation. The Son is only the Son because he is the Son to the Father. Without the Father he is not the Son, no more than the Father is the Father without the Son. The bond that unites them is from all eternity and to all eternity; it is peculiar to them. It is a bond of love since the very being of God is love. "I love my Father," Jesus says (John 14:31), echoing what God said at his baptism: "You are my well-beloved Son" (Mark 1:11).

There is no precedent in the Bible for what Jesus says about his bond with his disciples! The disciples might well be silent, as indeed they are! The bond they have with Jesus has only one model, the bond between Jesus and his Father! It is unheard of!

What more can I say, reader friend? To understand what Jesus says to us we have to understand his experience with his Father; we have to enter into this mystery, into the greatest depth of the mystery of "intradivine" intimacy . . . !

"Abide in me." Lord Jesus, what you are asking here is so mysterious to us! Neither is there any doubt that it is far beyond what we can manage! Have mercy upon us! How can we experience with you what you enjoy with your Father? We will never manage to be as close to you as you are to your Father! Yet you ask this of your disciples on the eve of your death, at the moment you are about to leave them and rejoin your Father! Don't abandon us to our inability to meet your expectation! Have pity upon us! If the pattern of what you ask is in heaven while we are on earth we will never manage to remain your disciples! Lord Jesus, we know what the bond can be between a father and his son and the son with his father, but you speak so differently of your communion with your Father, as no son has ever spoken of his father! How can we experience what we don't even understand? Have mercy on us, Lord! Take pity!

The perichōrēsis[6]

The bond of communion by mutual indwelling, which is the subject of Jesus' words, has no name in human languages because it does not exist upon the earth. Jesus himself has no specific word for it, but Christian theologians have proposed one for it in order to avoid lengthy circumlocutions; this is the word "perichōrēsis," and I will pick up on that

6. The OED defines this term as "theological" and meaning "circumincession." (Trans.)

here, not for the sake of appearing learned, but simply because it will help us see a little more clearly.

Etymologically speaking, perichōrēsis signifies "the fact of being around everything while also inside"! The word does say a lot, pointing to a glimpse we can have of a reality—and it is a reality, since Jesus speaks of it.

The word was not invented by the theologians but imported into the vocabulary, not from philosophy, but from dance! It is superb![7] It means that in the eyes of the theologians, the love relationship between the Father and the Son has something about it that suggests a dance! The perichōrēsis is a figure from dance in which each dancer finds himself turn and turn about on the outside and then the inside; this requires an unceasing movement in which each one steps back to give place to another, who then rushes in to replace him.

In so far as it concerns the divine persons, the perichōrēsis immediately took on a trinitarian dimension, describing the relationship of communion existing between the Father, the Son, and the Holy Spirit; the Holy Spirit too is "in" Christ and Christ is "in" him, as we discover for example in Luke's Gospel; he tells us in the same verse (4:1) that Jesus is "full" of the Holy Spirit, all the while being lead "in" the Holy Spirit. The reality of the perichōrēsis is truly a reality of the Trinity.

A marvelous aspect of this is the way the idea of the perichōrēsis leads us to think of God as in an eternal dance, an unceasing movement in which the three Persons efface themselves unendingly before each other, all the while stepping into the place left vacant. Indeed, God dances eternally! His very being, which is a constant surging of love, appears to our spirits as a never-ending dance, the dance of love of Father, Son, and Holy Spirit . . . .

Lord Jesus, I am full of wonderment before this divine reality, but how do you wish me to learn to live in you as you live in God? How can I, unless you teach me to live with you in this dynamic dance of love, with the beauty of movement you reveal, with the grace that is

---

7. The verb perichōrein means "to dance around."

yours, the perfection that is yours? How am I to love you, unceasingly effacing myself before you, giving place to you, and taking the place you leave me? How can I live on earth as you live in heaven? Lord Jesus Christ, Son of God, have mercy upon me, a sinner!

The double perichōrēsis

In response to our sense of inadequacy, indeed to forestall it, Jesus takes the lead. Before he asks his disciples to abide in him and he in them, before he invites them into his dance in this astonishing communion of love, Jesus takes time to make a statement to them which, rather than juxtaposing the two dances (the one of the Trinity, in heaven, and ours on earth with Christ), ties them together in one, since he himself, Jesus, takes part in both: "I in the Father and you in me and I in you" (John 14:20). Hence, to abide in Christ is to abide in perichōrēsis with him, since he himself is in perichōrēsis with the Father and the Holy Spirit. The divine pattern is not in heaven, far from us, but very near, as close as Christ, who includes us in himself. Blessed be God, who comes to our rescue!

But this is not all!

As Jesus specifies to his disciples in his long farewell discourse, there is also the question of the Father being "in" us (14:23) and the Spirit also being "in" us (14:17), which in turn causes us to be in the Father and in the Spirit. We are not abandoned to our own selves and our limitations, left to our blunders and failings; we are grasped by the Trinity in person, taken into the Trinity, carried along on the Trinity's wave of infinite love . . . .

In the account of the first four disciples' calling, we saw how Jesus involves us in a never-ending, surging movement of love, both towards God and others; here it becomes more precise; it is a movement with God, in God, as in a dance . . . .

The Trinity is not a mystery of love that is inaccessible to us, keeping us at arm's length, but a mystery that opens up to us, inviting us to enter in, into this love . . . . When Jesus came up from the baptismal waters, the heavens were opened, not only for his benefit, but for ours too; the Spirit descended on him, prefiguring his descent onto whoever is baptized into Christ. When Jesus walks along the shore of Galilee and invites us to follow him, he is inviting us to enter the divine dance and to fish for men with him, that they may also enter the dance . . . . Well may we bless his name!

No doubt a whole life is required to learn to live this profound communion of which Jesus speaks, a whole life to learn to love, to abide in this love, to dance like God, to dance with him, but there is no more beautiful approach to life than this . . . !

The Spirit abides

Who will teach us to abide in Christ today? Well, someone who already abides in him will, that is to say, his Father; Jesus himself says this (14:10) very simply—"we are one"! But who will help us understand what the Father teaches?

The very first uses of the word "abide" in John's Gospel are most instructive; more precisely, the first two uses, which occur together. Both are found on the lips of John the Baptist, the friend of the Bridegroom. Both have as their subject the Holy Spirit, and are in relation to Christ, who is the verb complement. Both refer back to the event of the baptism and are placed right at the heart of the mystery of the Trinity, at the moment the Holy Spirit comes down from heaven, from the Father to the Son.

Here is what John says after the baptism:

> I saw the Spirit descend from heaven like a dove and *abide* on him. As for me, I did not know him, but the one [= the Father] who sent me to baptize with water had told me,

"the one on whom you see the Spirit descend and *abide*, this is he who baptizes with the Holy Spirit." I have seen and borne witness that this is he, the Son of God. (John 1:32–34)

In both cases, it is the Spirit who "abides on" Christ. There is a subtle aspect to the two uses of the verb "abide" in that we don't know whether or not the Spirit *settled* on Christ. Did he abide above Jesus without settling on him, or did he indeed abide on him after settling there? It is impossible to say!

In Greek the verb for "abide" is a static verb; we can verify this in, for example, 19:31, where are told that the dead body of Jesus "remained on" the cross. There could be nothing more immobile than a body on a cross. Here, talking about the baptism, the same Evangelist uses the same verb with the same preposition ("on"), yet not this time with a dative (which would be correct for a static verb), but with an accusative, quite incorrectly, grammatically speaking, but with the effect of adding to this verb with no movement a nuance of movement; so the Spirit abides without movement but with momentum, both in movement and immobile! As is finely said by Narsai, a Syrian father, "The Spirit descends but without displacement." That says it very well! Did he settle and stay? Or didn't he? It is beyond expression, in the inexpressible mystery of communion proper to the persons of the Trinity.

We have seen previously the same type of situation with regard to the Son on the bosom of the Father, the same essence, the same movement within non-movement. In the same way as the Son is eternally in vital motion on the bosom of the Father, so the Spirit abides eternally in vital motion above the Son. The eternal descent of the Spirit onto the Son speaks again of the communion of trinitarian love. The Spirit is in eternal motion towards the Son; this is what John the Baptist "saw" on the day of the baptism, as the Father had previously announced to him.

The Baptist's vision _____

John the Baptist bears witness here to what he "saw" at the baptism! What exactly was it he saw? Further, does the verb "see" really fit with talking about this dynamic movement within the love of the Trinity?

According to the Evangelist's account, the Baptist seems to have been embarrassed to know which verb for "to see" he should use in describing his experience. The Evangelist himself does nothing to clarify the situation. What is going on here?

Our translations are unfortunately rather poor at rendering the Greek text; it is a little difficult to manage things differently because the language is lacking on the point that concerns us. In Greek, this passage juggles different verbs of seeing as it describes what the Baptist saw; what it says only finds a way into our linguistic categories with great difficulty.

Thus, in the passage, John is the subject of four different verbs for "to see": "seeing Jesus come" (*blepō*, v. 29), "I saw" (*theaomai*, v. 32), "you will see" (*idein*, v. 33), and "I saw" (*oraō*, v. 34).

When God says to the Baptist "you will see" (v. 33), he uses a verb that describes human vision: "you will see with your own human eyes." But when the Baptist says "I saw" (v. 32), he uses a verb more appropriate to the way God sees:[8] "I saw as God alone sees, with the eyes of God, things invisible to humans." Then as he recapitulates, he says that it is indeed with his human eyes that he saw what presented itself (v. 34). This uncertainty in John's mouth shows how far what he experienced at the baptism was beyond his understanding; he saw the invisible!

Everything the Baptist says is subsequent to Jesus' baptism. What really happened at the baptism itself? How does the Evangelist construct his narrative? How does he describe the scene and what does he have to say himself? The answer is that he does and says nothing, absolutely nothing! As strange as it might seem, the Evangelist is not

---

8. *Theaomai*, which the ancients derived from *theos*, God.

the author of the baptism account, of this fundamental event! He is content merely to report the witness of the Baptist.

Why this silence? Because it is simply beyond telling! Why so? Because it is the Trinity that is there contemplated by John the Baptist alone; the Father is there, the Son too, as well as the Holy Spirit . . . . No one can see or describe the Trinity! John the Evangelist prefers to be quiet, happy, in the paucity of his words, to simply report what the Baptist says.

The baptism of Jesus

At the outset of John's Gospel, the witness of the Baptist occupies a very important place. It is reported to us in two distinct phases, separated by the phrase "the next day" (1:29). Up to 1:28, the testimony reported corresponds very clearly (in line with the other three Gospels) to what the Baptist preached prior to Jesus' baptism: "make a straight path" (v. 23), "he comes after me" (v. 27), "I am not worthy to untie the straps of his sandals" (v. 27). What is said next, which we have already examined (1:32–34), comes after the baptism: "I saw the Spirit descend like a dove . . . ." The baptism is therefore in between the two, more precisely, between verses 28 and 29, so that the "next day," which opens verse 29, simply means, "the day of the baptism."

Jesus' baptism, in John's Gospel, therefore takes place in silence, between verses 28 and 29. The inexpressible is present in this silence! At the very moment the Evangelist could have told how the Trinity was manifest beside the Jordan, he says nothing. He lifts his pen from the page between the two verses and is silent, pondering . . . !

Though John does not recount the baptism itself, throughout his Gospel, in fact, he is at pains to convey the inexpressible mystery of the Trinity.

Following the Baptist's testimony, we understand that the heavens were opened above the Jordan, allowing the Father to gaze upon the Son, and the Son the Father, while the Spirit silently descends "without displacement" between the Father and the Son . . . . The heavens were open for a moment, allowing the Baptist to glimpse the indescribable theophany that belongs to eternity and that fills eternity.

The Baptist's testimony[9]

John, then, "saw"; John, the friend of the Bridegroom, whose joy is full; he who is the "greatest among men," as Jesus, his friend, says simply (Matt 11:11). After seeing, he made sure to leave an account, the testimony that the Evangelist received.

The Baptist is so overcome by the theophany of the baptism that he will then simply say of Jesus, "I didn't know him" (v. 31), whereas before the baptism he spoke of him as if he knew him very well, describing him in detail, with his axe, his winnowing fork in his hand, his power, his priestly majesty, his stature above that of the prophets. "You don't know him," he said to the crowd (John 1:26), indicating that the same was certainly not true of himself.

After the baptism, John's testimony is not at all what it was before. It is no longer a question of power, of an axe and a threshing floor, but of a lamb bearing the sin of the world! (vv. 29 and 36). Above all Jesus is presented as the Son of God (v. 34), where previously no such phrase had ever been used.

"I didn't know him," he insists, repeating it (vv. 31 and 33). How true! What did he know of the Son in his divinity? The answer is— nothing, not until the baptism, not until, as he looked at Christ, he gazed upon the Trinity. This is why, starting with "the next day," the Baptist's discourse is so altered; Christ takes on for him such a new dimension that he never even pronounces the name "Jesus"! Not once, while he lived, did this name appear on the Baptist's lips, though he

---

9. There is a much fuller account of the same passage in the author's book *Repentance—Good News!* (Trans.)

knew it well! He abstained from pronouncing it, just as he abstains from pronouncing the holy name of God! In this way, the Baptist testifies to the divinity of the one he recognized, that baptismal day, as "the Son of God."

Following the theophany of the baptism, John begins, in a way, to stammer! I believe that is the right word! He was so overcome by what he saw! Then, in a sentence that is a little confused, he lists three phrases that came to greatly illumine John the Evangelist: "This *is* he of whom I said, there *will come* after me one who precedes me because he *was* before me."

"He is, he is to come, he was . . . ." The Baptist is the first to employ these three verbal forms for the one person. He uses them without great emphasis, in a slightly confused sentence, and without knowing the impact they would have on the Evangelist, who, as we have seen, would make of them a designation for God as well as of Christ in his divinity: "He who is, who was, and who is to come."

After he contemplates the mystery of Christ and the mystery of the Trinity, John the Baptist retires into the wilderness, allowing his disciples to depart and follow his friend . . . . It required the immensity of the desert's silence to enfold this contemplative!

Abide in Christ

"Abide in me," says Jesus. What is it to "abide in him"? The only person who abides in him, our only point of reference, is the Father, according to the words of Jesus (John 14:10); Jesus adds no further commentary to this beyond stating the infinite love that unites them. We can add that the Holy Spirit "abides on him," as the Father himself says (1:33), and as the Baptist testifies (1:32); faced with the inexpressible no further precision is given here as to what "abide" means, except that the Spirit was "like a dove."

"The Father abides in me," the Son tells us, an expression suggesting no movement. "The Spirit abides on him," the Father tells us, an expression with movement . . . .

"To abide"; God alone knows what this means! Only in him, with him, and through him is this revealed to us, an unmoving movement, a stationary surge of energy, a great wave of love, infinite love. To abide is to continue, persevere, never cease to be within this eternal divine energy into which God alone can introduce us and then keep us and cause us to remain . . . . It is only in God that we can begin to experience all that in him is eternal. To help us with this, the Father and the Son send us the Spirit, who comes within us, preparing a place for the Father and the Son.

"The Spirit is in you," Jesus tells us (John 14:17); or, again, as certain manuscripts read, "he will be in you." The two phrases are equally true, stating as they do both the promise and its accomplishment, both absence and presence, the already and the not yet of participating in the perichoretic dance, in the eternal movement of love that characterize our relationship with God.

The Holy Spirit is very much in the background of the perichoretic formulations in John's Gospel, but there is more than enough said for us to understand that without him the harmony of the Trinity disappears. It's the Spirit who comes into us to open us up to the mystery of our communion with the Father and the Son, to illuminate it, to integrate us with it, to accomplish in us what Jesus says. It's the Spirit who enables us to know how to love and how to abide in this love, this love where the divine and the human work together, in synergy. He it is who reveals the presence of the Father and the Son in us, who prepares us for this and who immerses us in God, on the bosom of the Son and of the Father.

To abide is to continue in love, but not just any love. It is to continue in the love that originates and is fulfilled in the Father, that is experienced in the Son, that is animated by the Spirit, and that opens us up to others . . . and all this in an inexpressible movement of dance that overwhelms the capacity of human language!

After the cross

"Abide in me, and I in you," Jesus says on the eve of his death. Throughout the time of his incarnation, the disciples were only able to be "behind" or "alongside" him. It was impossible for them to be "in" Christ, just as it was impossible for Christ to be "in" them. For Christ to be able to be in his disciples, he had first to go away, which is to say, die. Before the cross, the perichōrēsis with Christ was not possible, but it became so after the cross and the resurrection.

After the cross everything is turned upside down; the perichōrēsis with Christ is possible, it becomes open to us, as does the perichōrēsis of the Trinity. This tells us the importance of the cross. After the cross, the divine perichōrēsis is open to us; the Trinity is no longer the same, since from that time it is given to us to be in God and for God to be in us, without either confusion or separation, just as the iron may be in the fire[10] and the fire in the iron, so that the iron becomes fire.

God in us and we in God; this has not been the case from all eternity, but only since the cross, though prepared from all eternity and to all eternity.

That they may be in us

The Spirit enters into us to enable us to abide in Christ. The Father too comes to make his abode in us to enable us to abide in his Son. Without God, this would be impossible.

10. The French has a nice play on words; *le fer est dans le feu.* The illustration of iron in fire is from the church fathers. (Trans.)

"Abide in me"; this command is always being addressed to us. We must endeavor to respond to the invitation, but never forgetting that Jesus, after his long farewell discourse, turns towards his Father and addresses a prayer to him in which he requests something inaccessible apart from God: "As you are in me and I am in you, may they be in us" (17:21). He asks this of the Father since he alone is able to convey us to this summit of communion in love, of which he is the source.

"That they may be perfectly one" (17:23); in this prayer, Christ uses the verb "to be" in a way that was altogether new to the disciples. He uses it with a particle followed by the accusative,[11] as if the verb "to be" had been transformed into a verb of motion. A characteristic of the divine nature is here being asked of the Father for the disciples; Father, that they may participate in our being. Christ goes the full distance in his love for us . . . .

To abide in Christ is to enter into a communion of love that goes far beyond our capacity because it is the communion of the Father, the Son, and the Holy Spirit. It is to enter this communion because Christ himself asks it of the Father, and the Father fulfills his Son's desires. It is to go right in and there abandon all our own love, and allow ourselves to be borne like a frail piece of bark floating on an immense river of love which takes infinite care of it, bearing it on towards the indescribable, where words no longer exist, because the river and the bark begin to dance for joy . . . .

11. Literally, "that they may be perfectly towards the one."

58543379R00073

Made in the USA
San Bernardino, CA
29 November 2017